1973
The Exmoor Handbook
and
Gazetteer

N. V. Allen

The Exmoor Press

MICROSTUDIES

Each Microstudy has been written by an expert and is designed to appeal to all who are interested in Exmoor.

The Editor of the Series is Victor Bonham-Carter.

A list of all the titles is available from

The Exmoor Press   Dulverton   Somerset

Printed in Great Britain by Cox, Sons & Co. Ltd., Williton, Somerset

Contents

Illustrations

Pull-out Map	Beryl Campbell
Architectural and Landscape Drawings	Sidney Perrin
Flower Drawings	Audrey Bonham-Carter
Photographs (except where stated otherwise)	Colin Thornton
Cover: Exford's Signpost to the Moor	Colin Thornton

Orthography

The spelling of Place Names agrees with that shown on the special Exmoor Tourist One-Inch Ordnance Survey Map. The Map References in the Gazetteer have also been drawn from this source.

The Author

N. V. Allen has also written *Birds of Exmoor* in the Microstudy Series, where a brief biographical note will be found.

Acknowledgments

The author acknowledges with many thanks information given him by county officials of Devon and Somerset, by the National Trust, and by Colonel B. Cocks, of the Exmoor Information Centre, Minehead. Needless to say, the views expressed are his own. Once again he is especially grateful to his wife, Marjorie, for help in checking the manuscript and proofs.

1 Exmoor—Facts and Figures

The National Park

Ever since Wordsworth and Coleridge walked the hills above
Dunster to Lynmouth and the Valley of the Rocks, the natural
beauty of West Somerset and North Devon has been recognised and
praised. From the early 19th century onwards, a growing number of
visitors has been attracted by the grandeur of the rugged coastline,
the fine, clear, sweeps of open moorland, and the numerous streams
that race down the hillsides, through lonely combes, and by lovely
villages, on their way to the sea. So it was not surprising when, in
1954, this unique region—with its wealth of wild life and natural
beauty—was designated a National Park.

Since Exmoor lies in two counties, the administration is divided.
There is a Devon National Park Committee and a Somerset National
Park Committee, and a Joint Advisory Committee. Both the
Devon and Somerset Committees exercise planning powers under
the authority of their County Councils, while the Joint Advisory
Committee co-ordinates policy. Although cumbrous, the system
works tolerably well—despite a serious flaw in National Parks
legislation which failed, at the outset, to clarify the divergent
interests of those who own, use and enjoy the wild and open spaces:
be they farmers, foresters, naturalists, sportsmen, or visitors.
Some progress, however, has been made towards finding reasonable
answers to this problem and, with continuing goodwill, it now
seems likely that the greater part of Exmoor's surviving moorland
is safe from further erosion and enclosure. Under the Local
Government Act, 1972, it is expected that a single Committee, made
up of members from both Somerset and Devon, will administer
the Park as from April 1974.

When so much of 'England's green and pleasant land' has been
marred by urban spread, this corner of the country remains a
priceless heritage for the enjoyment of all. A debt of gratitude
is due to many for its safe keeping: to government and county
authorities who exercise statutory control over it; to owners and
occupiers who are committed to its care and use; to private people
and societies, without whose foresight and vigilance much of
its value might have been lost; and to the local Press for its sustained
interest and wise reporting.

Area and Boundary

Exmoor National Park covers an area of 265 square miles, or some 170,000 acres, of which about two-thirds are in Somerset, and the rest in Devon. 17,000 acres, or 10%, is woodland, some 43,000 acres, or 26%, is open moorland, and the balance is mostly grassland for the maintenance of horses, cattle, and thousands of sheep. Only in the Porlock Vale, which curves round to Timberscombe and Dunster, is there any extensive arable land where corn and root crops are grown.

The northern boundary is formed by a coastline of high, rugged cliffs, extending for 29 miles from the outskirts of Minehead to Combe Martin. From this Devon seaside village the boundary runs diagonally across country to Dulverton, taking in Kentisbury Down, Challacombe, and Twitchen. Just below Dulverton it turns north-eastwards to cut across Haddon Hill and on to Raleigh's Cross on the Brendons. From here it continues almost due east to Elworthy before returning to Minehead via Monksilver, Withycombe, and Dunster. Total length of the boundary is about 100 miles. The Exmoor National Park sign—an outlined stag's head in black on a green triangle—has been set up by many of the roads where they enter the Park.

Physical Features

Half of Exmoor is a high plateau lying from 1,000 to 1,600 feet above sea level, with heather and grass moors as the dominant vegetation. Dunkery Beacon at 1,705 feet is the highest point, Five Barrows, at Span Head, is 1,618 feet, Chains Barrow, on The Chains, 1,599 feet, and the highest part of the Brendons is Lype Hill at 1,390 feet. This Exmoor plateau, with the Brendons forming the eastern, and Holdstone Down and Hangman the western section, is broken up by the rivers Barle, Exe, the deep gorges of the East Lyn and Heddon, and by numerous streams and combes. These pierce and scar all the high land, especially towards the north and around Dulverton. There are good stretches of sandy beaches from Dunster to Minehead, otherwise the shore-line consists largely of pebbles and rocky outcrops. The long range of hog-back cliffs, topping nearly 1,000 feet in places, are among the highest in Britain, and can best be appreciated from a boat.

Almost the whole of Exmoor is composed of Devonian and Old Red Sandstone rocks, except in the northern part where there are beds of Triassic or New Red Sandstone. In places these rocks give the soil and the local building stone the characteristic reddish colour. Near Selworthy there is a strip of Lias rocks consisting of limestone and shales, and the low lying ground near Porlock and east of Minehead contains sands, pebbles, and clays of the Recent Period.

Ownership and Access

Public and similar organisations hold the following areas of the National Park, otherwise Exmoor is almost entirely privately owned.

SOMERSET COUNTY COUNCIL

North Hill, Minehead	600 acres	
Hawkcombe Valley, Porlock	240 ,,	
Mill Hill, Oare	300 ,,	
The Chains, Driver and Pinkworthy Farms	2,000 ,,	
		3,140

NATIONAL TRUST

Holnicote Estate, Selworthy	12,420 acres	
Winsford Hill and Tarr Steps	1,290 ,,	
Lyn Valley	508 ,,	
Heddon Valley and Trentishoe Down	850 ,,	
Woody Bay	115 ,,	
Foreland Point, Countisbury	705 ,,	
		15,888

FORESTRY COMMISSION

Brendon Hills		3,033 acres	
East Down, Brayford	approx.	100 ,,	
			3,133

Grand Total	22,161

The moorland and woodland belonging to the Somerset County Council, National Trust, and Forestry Commission are open to the public to wander at will, except where there may be some restriction in newly planted woodland. Owners of other open moorland areas rarely object to the public walking or picnicing on their land. But always remember to keep dogs away from grazing sheep, and remove all your litter. On farmland keep to the paths, for grass is a valuable crop, fasten all gates, and avoid damage to walls and fences. Farmers are busy men in the summer months, but are used to having visitors around, and they have a reputation for being helpful and friendly.

Communications

Until the arrival of the railways the bulkier goods were conveyed by ships to the little harbours. Records going back to the 13th century tell of this sea-borne traffic to Watchet, Minehead, Porlock, and Ilfracombe. Coal was landed at Porlock Weir as late as 1950, while Watchet is still busy with ships bringing in regular cargoes. Trading, however, has ceased elsewhere in the region. None the less the harbours remain attractive centres of interest, with fishing and pleasure boats, yachts, and the summer steamers of the White Funnel line. See Grahame Farr's Microstudy, *Ships and Harbours of Exmoor*.

No fewer than eight railways sprang up round Exmoor between 1865 and 1900, but all are now closed except for the short Lynmouth-Lynton cliff railway.   The final Exmoor closure by British Railways was the Taunton-Minehead line in January 1971, but strenuous efforts are still being made by enthusiasts to have this re-opened as a private venture.   Trains still serve the larger towns on the outskirts of Exmoor with stations at Bridgwater, Taunton, and Barnstaple. See Robin Madge's Microstudy, *Railways Round Exmoor*.

Four main roads lead into the Exmoor region, with the A.361 running along the south border from Taunton to Bampton, South Molton, and Barnstaple, and the A.39 following the north coast from Minehead to Lynmouth before swinging inland to Barnstaple. The A.396 Bampton to Dunster road crosses the National Park in the south to north direction.   None of these roads can be considered fast, as they all have sections with tricky bends, and for most of the way carry only one line of traffic in each direction.   There are also four good B roads, otherwise many of the villages and hamlets are connected by narrow, country lanes.

At present these are adequate for the local winter traffic but become very busy, occasionally overcrowded, in the summer months.   Major problems will arise with the completion of the M.5 motorway, when it is expected that the number of people living within $3\frac{1}{2}$ hours driving time of Exmoor will increase from the present 5 million to nearly 18-19 million.   This new motorway will roughly follow the line of the present A.38 from Bristol to Exeter, but passing just south of Bridgwater, Taunton, and Wellington, and within 20 miles of Exmoor.   The Somerset section of the M.5 is expected to be completed by the end of 1975.

National Park authorities have plans afoot to meet a vastly increased influx of day visitors, and those coming off the motorway will be encouraged to follow Tourist Routes.   These will be sign-posted to pass through some of Exmoor's loveliest country, but it is hoped that large parts of the moors will be kept as quiet areas for walkers, horse riders, and naturalists.   Future projects include the publication of a specialised tourist map of Exmoor, an enlarged Warden advice service, and the building of new feeder roads, picnic areas, car parks, view points, and toilets.

Population

The number of residents living within the National Park today is about 12,500.   This figure does not include the Urban District of Minehead (Pop. 8,063), which was excluded from the Park, or Combe Martin (Pop. 2,420), where the main area of population also lies outside.   Exmoor contains no big towns, and nothing larger than a fair-sized village.   The most populated places are Lynton combined with Lynmouth, 1,981; Dulverton 1,392; Porlock 1,307. Among the smaller parishes are Countisbury 80; Oare 57; Trentishoe 47; Treborough 44; Culbone 27.

The population trend is for the inland villages to show a steady decline, and the coastal resorts and parishes an increase, though this seems to have been halted in the case of Lynton and Porlock. Some inland parishes have shown a drastic decrease in the 30 years from 1931 to 1961: Winsford 534 to 363; Withypool 303 to 252; Cutcombe 420 to 330; Culbone 43 to 27; Luxborough 274 to 182. Over the same period the Dulverton Rural District dropped from 5,021 to 4,020, with Dulverton itself losing about 100. All the parish populations are given in the Gazetteer, and the popularity of Minehead is evident from the sample table given below.

	1801	1851	1901	1951	Latest
Brendon	260	265	262	283	213
Challacombe	158	289	195	147	153
Combe Martin	819	1,441	1,521	2,301	2,420
Lynton/Lynmouth	481	1,059	1,641	2,123	1,981
Minehead	1,168	1,420	3,459	7,401	8,063
Oare	64	57	80	61	57
Parracombe	322	460	315	368	309
Porlock	600	854	651	1,479	1,307
Treborough	132	115	123	63	44

Climate and Rainfall

Conditions are certainly mild on Exmoor, snow only occasionally settles along the coast, though regularly for short periods on the high moorland. On average, heavy and prolonged snow occurs every tenth year, while every seventh year is more than usually wet. Winds can be strong from the west, and a gale on Chapman Barrows or Span Head can be leaned against. From early spring to the end of autumn it is normal to have many weeks of delightful sunshine, interspersed with short periods of rain and low cloud. Fog seldom lingers, but misty conditions may develop suddenly on high ground. Should anyone be lost in a mist, the best plan is to find a stream and follow it down. This is sure to lead to lower and clearer ground.

The most notable feature about the Exmoor climate is the varied amounts of rainfall. Around Minehead the yearly average is 35 inches, at Dulverton 60 inches, and on the exposed Chains 80 inches. Otherwise the weather can best be described as 'satisfactory for all concerned', for quite a mixture is needed by those who look to Exmoor for their outdoor recreation. The huntsman prefers a good shower of rain from time to time to improve the scent; a long dry spell best suits the rambler, birdwatcher, and ordinary holiday-maker; the dinghy sailors at Minehead and Porlock look for clear weather and a fresh breeze; a calm, dull drizzle is ideal for the fishermen. Most of these conditions prevail over an average Exmoor summer.

Information—Where to find it

OFFICES

When applying for literature through the post, remember to enclose the cost of return postage.

EXMOOR NATIONAL PARK

See Combe Martin, Dulverton, Exeter, Minehead, and Taunton below.

NATIONAL TRUST

Information Centre and Shop is on the Holnicote Estate, the postal address being Selworthy, Minehead. The Centre is signposted on the main A.39 from Minehead, some two miles from Porlock. Open throughout the year. A wide range of Exmoor literature is available.

BARNSTAPLE

Town guide distributed by the Town Clerk's department, Civic Centre. Exmoor literature is available at The Athenaeum, Barnstaple's fine museum.

COMBE MARTIN

Devon County Council has a well equipped Information Centre in the main Harbour Car Park. Open daily from Easter to October, 10 a.m. to 4.0 p.m. Combe Martin Publicity Association issues an attractive little guide, and deals with postal enquiries throughout the year.

DULVERTON

Information on local matters is supplied either through the post or to callers at the Rural District Council Office, Exmoor House. The offices of the Exmoor Society are in the Parish Rooms, High Street, and open to the public on Tuesday and Saturday, 10.30 a.m. to 12.30 p.m. Literature about the National Park, the Society and Exmoor generally is available.

EXETER

Literature on Exmoor can be obtained from the County Planning Officer, County Hall.

ILFRACOMBE

Town Information Office in Western Promenade.

LYNTON/LYNMOUTH

Lyn Publicity Association runs an Information Bureau in Lee Road, Lynton, for callers and postal enquiries. Open 10.0 a.m. to 1.0 p.m. and 3.0 p.m. to 4.0 p.m.

MINEHEAD

Here, in The Parade, is the main Exmoor Information Office, open throughout the year. An expert officer is also present from Easter to October.

In the same building the Minehead Publicity Association has its Information Bureau, and issues the town guide.

PORLOCK

The Information Centre is located in Mr. Lynn's ironmongery shop in the High Street. Information and accommodation leaflets in English, French, and German are available free of charge to callers during normal shop hours, or through the post.

SOUTH MOLTON

Guides and information can be obtained from the Council Offices, 8, East Street.

TAUNTON

Literature on Exmoor can be obtained from the County Planning Officer, County Hall.

MUSEUMS

BARNSTAPLE. The North Devon Athenaeum in The Square has fine geological and botanical sections, and an excellent reference library.

ILFRACOMBE. There is a small museum of general interest near the seafront.

LYNTON. Lyn Exmoor Museum in the old Vincent Cottage has an interesting collection of local bye-gones.

MALMSMEAD. A small Lorna Doone museum at Lorna Doone Farm.

MINEHEAD. An interesting Exmoor Gallery at the Information Centre, Market House, The Parade.

SOUTH MOLTON. The museum is housed in the Guildhall, and includes several old fire engines, documents and relics of the Borough's history, all attractively displayed. Also a good collection of minerals mined in the district.

TAUNTON. The Somerset County Museum, and the offices of the Somerset Archaeological and Natural History Society, are located in Taunton Castle near the centre of the town.

LIBRARIES

Both the Devon and Somerset County Councils maintain a fine library service within the National Park. In addition to the centres listed below, they each operate three travelling libraries with a total of some 800 stopping places.

BARNSTAPLE, The Square. Open each weekday except Tuesday afternoon.

BRAUNTON, Chaloners Road. Open each weekday except Tuesday afternoon.

COMBE MARTIN, Westbourne Terrace. Open Monday and Tuesday afternoon; all day Wednesday and Friday; Saturday morning.

DULVERTON, Lady Street. Open Tuesday afternoon; all day Friday; and Saturday morning.

ILFRACOMBE, Brookfield Place.   Open each weekday except Wednesday afternoon.

MINEHEAD, Bancks Street.   Open each weekday except Wednesday.

PORLOCK, High Street.   Open Tuesday afternoon and all day Friday.

SOUTH MOLTON, East Street.   Open each weekday except Tuesday, and Saturday afternoon.

WATCHET, The Esplanade.   Open Tuesday afternoon, and all day Thursday and Saturday.

WILLITON, Long Street.   Open Monday, Wednesday, and Friday afternoons only.

LOCAL PAPERS

The West Somerset Free Press, Long Street, Williton, has the widest Exmoor coverage, and reports local events in depth.   Weekly on Friday.

The North Devon Journal-Herald, 96, High Street, Barnstaple, covers the Lynton, Combe Martin, Ilfracombe, and Barnstaple districts. Weekly on Thursday.

Somerset County Gazette, Castle Green, Taunton, covers much of West Somerset and Taunton in particular.   Weekly on Fridays.

The Exmoor Review, Parish Rooms, Dulverton.   The journal of the Exmoor Society.   Annually in December.

Tarr Steps.

2 Landscape

Looking down upon a relief map of Exmoor—and there is a very good one in the Minehead Information Centre—three physical features stand out: *the high moorland,* much of it above 1,250 feet; *the deeply-cut valleys* running down from this central highland, and usually narrow and wooded in their lower reaches; and *the rugged line of cliffs* falling abruptly into the Bristol Channel. These features are remarkably well distributed over the whole of the National Park, and the chief holiday resorts from Minehead to Combe Martin each have a cross-section of this glorious scenery on their very doorsteps. Inland—Dulverton, Winsford, Exford, and Simonsbath are all situated along river banks amid unspoiled countryside. No part is more than 17 miles from the sea.

Moorland and the Royal Forest

The 43,500 acres of open moorland includes all the high ground except the Brendon Hills, where much of the heathland has been planted with conifers within the present century. The principal vegetation of the moorland areas is heather, mainly *Calluna Vulgaris,* western gorse, *Ulex Gallii,* and a coarse stiff grass, *Molinia Caerulea,* called 'flying bent' or purple moor grass—so-called because, becoming brittle in the autumn, the leaves are snapped off by strong winds and blown into the ditches. Large clumps of rush, notably *Juncus Effusus,* flourish on wet land; likewise the common cotton grass, *Eriophorum Angustifolium,* found on the northern slopes of Dunkery, around Larkbarrow, Moles Chamber, and on The Chains, where there are also about 150 acres of deer sedge, *Scirpus Cespitosus.*

Heather moorland is dominant on Dunkery, Winsford Hill, Withypool Common, Molland Moor, in parts of the Brendons to the east, and on Trentishoe and Holdstone Downs along the coast. Grass moorland commands the landscape around Swap Hill and Black Barrow above Oare, in the hilly six-mile stretch from Brendon Two Gates to Chapman Barrows, and from Hangley Cleave to Shoulsbarrow Castle south of Simonsbath. Much of this grassland lies within the old Royal Forest of Exmoor (see Chapter 3)—the result, it is believed, of extensive sheep grazing since the Middle Ages, which destroyed the natural heather. The general treelessness of Exmoor in the past is emphasised by the survival of two tree names: Hoar Oak on Hoar Oak Water, where its successor still stands by the Forest Wall; and Kite Oak, no longer extant but its site above Chalk Water is corrupted to Kittuck. Both served as Forest boundary marks. See Geoffrey Sinclair's Microstudy, *The Vegetation of Exmoor.*

Rivers and their Valleys

Exmoor has three main rivers—the Barle, Exe, and the Lyn; five minor ones—the Haddeo, east of Dulverton; the Quarme, below Wheddon Cross and which joins the Exe at Exton; the Avill, that flows through Dunster; Badgeworthy Water, for much of its course the boundary between Somerset and Devon; and the Heddon, which runs swiftly through Parracombe and Hunter's Inn to the Bristol Channel. In addition, and forming one of the chief glories of Exmoor, there are numerous delightful streams, full of lively brown trout, and the home country of the charming dipper and grey wagtail. These streams include Chetsford Water above Porlock, running into Nutscale reservoir to supply Minehead; Horner Water rising out of Dunkery beyond Cloutsham, and gurgling through shady oak woodlands to Bossington and the sea; Danes Brook, flowing beneath Hawkridge before joining the Barle; and Weir and Chalk Waters which unite with Badgeworthy Water at Malmsmead in the heart of the Doone country, to form the East Lyn river.

RIVER BARLE

PINKWORTHY TO SIMONSBATH

This emerges from Pinkworthy Pond, 1,400 feet up on the western edge of The Chains, and flows through Simonsbath, Withypool and Dulverton, before joining the Exe at Exebridge just beyond the National Park. Its total length is about 30 miles, and to many people is the most attractive of the Exmoor rivers, though lovers of the Exe and Lyn will strongly deny this. Pinkworthy (pronounced Pinkery) Pond can easily be reached from the Simonsbath-Challacombe road by a steady uphill walk of about two miles. This can be continued to include Wood Barrow (1,566 feet), Longstone Barrow, the famous Longstone, and Chapman Barrows (1,574 feet) to the west, or to Chains Barrow (1,599 feet) and Exe Head, the source of the River Exe, to the east. The most distant of these places is some three miles further on from Pinkworthy Pond, and brings the walker into the more remote parts of Exmoor.

Pinkworthy Pond is a small artificial lake constructed for John Knight in about 1850, by a party of Irish workmen, possibly as a reservoir for a canal (never built). Today, it covers about four acres, and is 30 feet deep by the retaining wall. It was the scene of a tragedy in 1880 when a young farmer drowned himself in the pond. The Barle is only a small stream when it flows by Pinkworthy Farm and on past several rocky mounds to go under the Simonsbath—Challacombe road. The farmhouse has recently been colour-washed pink, and adapted by the Somerset Education Authority as a centre for outdoor school activities. For about a mile the infant Barle runs parallel to the road where there are wide verges for parking and picnics. It then turns inland behind Cornham Farm, and runs through a little known but picturesque valley before emerging again close to Simonsbath. By now it has received the waters of many streams from the combes of the high ridge of Setta Barrow (1,555 feet), Burcombe, and Moles Chamber.

River Barle at Simonsbath.

SIMONSBATH, COW CASTLE, LANDACRE BRIDGE

To follow the Barle from Simonsbath to Landacre Bridge, a distance of 5½ miles, take the path through the bottom end of the wood opposite the Exmoor Forest Hotel. Despite its name, Birch Cleave, here are some magnificent *beech* trees, a living memorial to the Knight family, who planted them over a hundred years ago. Beyond the wood the path continues for a while, but then peters out on the steep bracken slopes. Thence as far as Cow Castle the route is often wet and difficult, passing the site of the Wheal Eliza copper and iron mine to be mentioned in the next chapter.

Cow Castle, an Iron Age fortress on the north bank of the river, is about half-way between Simonsbath and Landacre Bridge. It can be more easily reached by walking up the right-hand side from Landacre. The Castle stands in a commanding position, some 300 feet high, and with a circular 10-foot earth rampart round the rocky summit. A legend credits the work to a band of hardy moorland fairies, and it was long known as Ring Castle. Alongside is a smaller mound named The Calf. From here on the Barle continues past a fir plantation, and in a widening valley to the old five-span bridge at Landacre.

Withypool Bridge.

WITHYPOOL AND TARR STEPS

The next 2½ miles to Withypool is the least picturesque section of the river, though there is always the chance of seeing a kingfisher, or a pair of common sandpipers. The public right-of-way lies along the south bank, but walking through grass fields can be wet and muddy in places. Withypool is a very old moorland village and there is a Domesday reference to three 'foresters of Widepolla'. Men from Withypool were early employed on Forest duties, but nowadays the resident population has sharply declined, and the place has an empty isolated air. It possesses a pleasant inn, a fine bridge, and an attractive grey stone church.

Below Withypool and all the way to Dulverton, a distance of 10 miles, the Barle resumes all its delightful features. Here is riverside walking at its very best, along paths winding through oak woodlands, peaceful and secluded amid a variety of wild life and flowers. Tarr Steps spans the Barle four miles below Withypool, but is usually approached by the narrow road which leads down from Winsford Hill. There is a large free car park, with toilets, 500 yards before the river is reached. Refreshments are available at a farmhouse overlooking Tarr Steps. This is really a causeway for use by men and packhorses, rather than a bridge, and consists of stone slabs resting on piers three feet above the water. Together with a paved approach it is 180 feet long, and is the finest stone causeway of its kind in the British Isles. Experts differ as to its age, but it is certainly not later than the 13th century, and may belong to the Iron Age period, 300 B.C. Severe flooding has damaged it from time to time, but careful restoration has always been carried out.

After Tarr Steps the Barle flows below Hawkridge, a tiny village set up on a ridge, and is joined by the Danes Brook near to Brewer's and Mounsey Castles, which long ago guarded a ford at the junction. These old earth forts, in dense woodland on the north bank of the river, are now difficult to locate in the thick undergrowth. Hawkridge, like all the moorland villages except Simonsbath, is an ancient place, and the church has a fine Norman doorway.

A mile before Dulverton, the B.3223 joins the Barle, and they travel together into the busy little town. Lord Tennyson and his son visited Dulverton and villages around in the 1890s, and his son has left an account of their visit:

'In the afternoon we drove through the Barle valley to Hawkridge, then to Tarr Steps, high up amongst the hills, with an ancient bridge across the river, flat stones laid on piers. Some tawny cows were cooling themselves in mid-stream; a green meadow on one side, on the other a wooded slope. "If it were only to see this", my father said, "the journey is worthwhile".'

The Barle then flows on for another couple of miles, before joining the Exe at Blackpool, near Exebridge.

RIVER EXE

The country surrounding the river Exe has hardly changed since W. H. Hudson traced its course 70 years ago, and left this impression in Chapter 23 of his book, *Afoot in England.*

'Many rivers have I seen in my wanderings, but never one to compare with this visionary river, which yet existed, and would be found and followed at last. My forefathers had dwelt for generations beside it, listening all their lives long to its music, and when they left it they still loved it in exile.'

On the vast uplifted Chains, some two miles east of Pinkworthy Pond, a peaty bog continually oozes water to form first a trickle, and then a stream running in a deep gully. This is Exehead, a wild and barren spot, described by Edward Hutton in his *Highways and Byways of Somerset* as:

'A bare rolling waste very like the sea, with its long heaving monotony of grey water, without a voice, without life, and without human habitation; there is only the sound of wind and of running water. That is the moor, and its face is the face of eternity.'

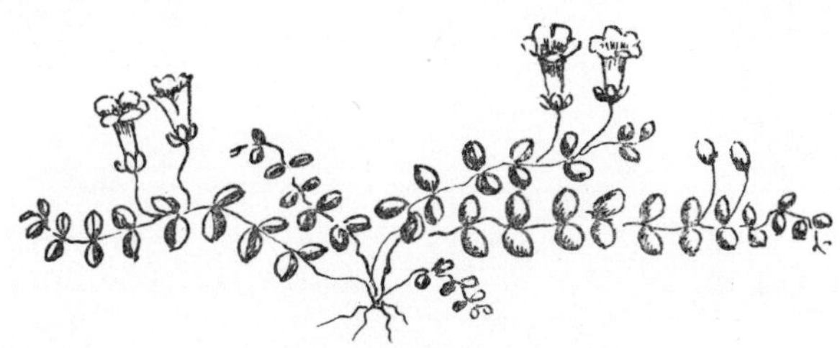

Bog Pimpernel

The Exe flows only as a stream under the Simonsbath—Lynton road, but gathering strength from the waters of Elsworthy and Wellshead, it enters Exford as a youthful river. This is another Domesday village, curiously fragmented today, with its centre in the valley and houses stretching along all the roads out of it. The church stands on its own up the hill. Sport is an important activity. Here are the kennels of the Devon and Somerset Staghounds, stretches of good fishing, and plenty of scope for the tourists—be they patrons of the hotels and cafes, or ramblers stopping at the youth hostel. A discerning visitor will be delighted by the two stained glass windows by Burne Jones in the Methodist Chapel.

From Exford there is another fine riverside path, mainly through meadows, for much of the way to Winsford. At one point it is necessary to divert at Court House up to Higher Combe, and rejoin the river at Lyncombe. Almost all the way the moorland towers overhead on every hand. Staddon Hill to the north, and Road Hill to the south of the river. Both are over 1,000 feet high and have remains of early hill forts. Here the Barle and the Exe are little more than a mile apart until the great mass of Winsford Hill (1,404 feet) forces them asunder just before the village is reached.

Winsford may well be the prettiest village on Exmoor, with six bridges large and small, spanning the Exe and its tributaries within 500 yards of the village green. During 1929 road and bridge reconstruction work was carried out, but not without angry protests from the residents at this 'extravagent, wholesale, vandalistic road widening', Apart from an unusually broad but pleasant approach into the village from Coppleham Cross, this attack on its seclusion and charm passes unnoticed today.

Beyond Coppleham Cross, with its heronry of some twenty nests, to the southern tip of the National Park, the Exe runs through a wooded valley parallel to the Minehead—Exeter road, A.396. On their way the river and road pass beneath the hamlet of Exton, perched up on a rocky hillside. The setting is delightful, but there is little to see apart from the old church with traces of Norman masonry. Included within the parish is Bridgetown, which boasts a fine cricket pitch and thatched pavilion on the banks of the Exe. Parking space allows the passing motorist to pull in for a few overs whenever there is a home match.

Just before the deer sanctuary of Barlynch, there are the remains of an abbey of that name, lying between the river and the road. A community of Cistercian friars lived here until they were dispersed at the Reformation. Mention is made of it in the Third Perambulation of Exmoor Forest in 1298, 'the priory of Barlich with woods, heaths and appertenances which the Prior of Barlich holds'. Some of the stones from the ruins have been used for the building of a nearby cottage and farmstead.

This final stretch of the Exe before its union with the Barle at Exebridge is of great beauty, winding between high wooded banks, a favourite resort of the red deer, fox, and many smaller mammals and birds. On the Dulverton side of the river is Pixton Hill (779 feet) and Pixton Park, once the home of the Earl of Carnarvon. Arthur Mee calls this Exe valley road, 'one of the most impressive in Somerset'. So the river Exe, having begun as a trickle in a barren waste only to be discovered after a strenuous walk, leaves the National Park in this idyllic setting beside a main road.

THE LYN RIVERS

There are two main branches of the river Lyn, the East and the West, and they only unite near the centre of Lynmouth village less than 500 yards from the sea. Previous to this junction they both run as mountain torrents—the name Lyn probably comes from a Saxon word, *hlynna*, meaning a torrent—through steeply wooded valleys, full of light and shade and sound of hurrying waters. Here are lots of brown trout and leaping salmon in their season. A favourite spot on this lower section is the delightful walk up to Watersmeet where Hoaroak, flowing down from The Chains, meets the East Lyn travelling from Brendon and Oare.

Many Exmoor waters combine to form the East Lyn river, and its source can be traced to the boggy Meads beneath Alderman's Barrow, only three miles from Exford. Here among the rushes growing out of a peaty soil is the head of Chalk Water, a stream that winds through lovely moorland country to Oareford, where it links up with Weir Water, familiar to all who picnic beside Robber's Bridge. Between Oareford and Malmsmead in Doone country, the widening stream is called Oare Water. Then, right on the Devon border, Badgeworthy Water flows in and the East Lyn river is named at last. Below Malmsmead, the river runs at an unhurried pace, and almost lingers in front of the cottages and inn at Brendon, before it disappears into Barton Wood to gather speed for its final descent to Lynmouth and the sea.

The West Lyn takes a less spectacular course, but its headwaters are 1,500 feet up on The Chains, and only just over the crest from Pinkworthy Pond, source of the river Barle. The river leaves the old Royal Forest of Exmoor by Ruckham Combe on Thorn Hill, and is fed by numerous streams all the way to the hamlet of Barbrook. From here onwards, the river and road wind all the way together through a wooded valley to Lynmouth.

It scarcely seems possible that a valley so perfect and charming in its sylvan setting, could be the scene of devastation and disaster. But such it was on the night of Friday, 15th August, 1952, when after hours of heavy rain on Exmoor, millions of tons of water poured off the moor into the valleys below. Nothing could withstand such a torrent; trees, bridges, buildings, roads, vehicles, everything in its path was swept away. Thirty-four people lost their lives, including eleven visitors on holiday, and the material damage was estimated at £2 million.

The main cause of the disaster was the unparalleled amount of rain on Exmoor, especially on The Chains, where 9 inches fell in less than 24 hours. During the preceding two weeks rainfall had been quite heavy with $3\frac{1}{2}$ inches recorded. This had already saturated the ground, and no more could be absorbed when the mighty deluge began on the 15th, and water a foot deep was driven across the moor into the combe below. It was the most violent storm ever known in the west of England.

Every effort has now been made to guard against heavy flooding in the future. Thousands of tons of debris have been removed from the Lyn, the bed straightened and widened, and banks strengthened. The scars of the tragedy have long been removed, and Lynmouth remains a seaside village of character and charm.

Coastal Region

Twenty-nine miles of coastline stretching from Minehead to Combe Martin forms the northern border of Exmoor National Park. There are steep rugged cliffs all the way apart from a 2-mile break along the stony beach in Porlock Bay, and brief river gaps at Lynmouth and Heddon's Mouth. In many places the ground in this coastal region rises well above 1,000 feet, and the middle section on the main Porlock—Lynmouth road, A.39, reaches almost 1,400 feet. This accounts for the stiff climb up Porlock Hill, and the corresponding descent down Countisbury Hill. Except for the shores of the holiday resorts, or where there are well defined paths, none of the isolated beaches can be safely reached. The cliffs are treacherous to climb, and there is always the hazard of being cut off by the tide. This Exmoor coast has the finest scenery in Britain, but it cannot be over emphasized that it is for viewing, and not for climbing.

MINEHEAD AND THE NORTH HILL

The urban district of Minehead was excluded from the National Park, yet it remains the chief gateway to Exmoor. Formerly the town had three distinct sections which are still traceable—Quay Town, Lower Town, and Upper or Church Town. Below the church of St. Michael, which stands well up on North Hill, are

Dunster Yarn Market and Castle.

Combe Martin Bay.

The Barle Valley from Wheal Eliza

The Hoar Oak.

The Longstone.

narrow lanes, old houses, buildings and steps of the early Upper Town. Lovers of old books will find great delight in the beautiful illuminated missal of the 14th century exhibited in the church.

Behind Minehead a road winds up to the top of North Hill, and continues for 4 miles along the crest to Selworthy Beacon. This is a splendid scenic road, passing over moorland owned by Somerset County Council, and the National Trust, and has magnificent panoramic views in every direction. Selworthy Beacon (1,013 feet) is the end of the motor road, but footpaths lead on to Hurlstone Point, down to the beach, and through the woods to the cluster of old-world villages of Bossington, Selworthy, and Allerford. These are all beautiful places, but each has distinctive features. Allerford has a packhorse bridge; Selworthy an ancient church and tithe barn, and thatched cottages; Bossington, quaint dwellings with tall round chimneys, the Lynch chapel of ease restored by Sir Thomas Acland from a barn in 1884, and some large walnut trees.

THE THREE PORLOCKS

The name means 'the enclosed harbour', which indicates its former maritime status, though the main village is now separated from the sea by a mile-wide stretch of meadow and marshland. There is much of interest in the parish church dedicated to St. Dubricius, Bishop of Llandaff, who crossed over from Glamorgan about the year 600 to bring the Gospel to the Exmoor region. Some recumbent effigies are especially noteworthy, and one of John Harington, a knight of Agincourt, and his wife, is the finest of its kind in England. The village has many old cottages with tall curious chimneys that back on to the roadway, so built as to prevent prying eyes seeing in during the troubled days of Charles I. At the Ship Inn near the fork of the road to Porlock Weir, the poet Southey was detained during a rainy day, and wrote a sonnet to while away the hours.

Midway between Porlock and Porlock Weir stands a cluster of houses forming West Porlock. This is an early settlement, and the old forge is now a carefully designed cottage. In the grounds stands the former thatched lock-up, and this juxtaposition of forge and prison was handy for shackling prisoners. Just beyond, the left fork of the road winds on to Worthy Manor, beautifully set between woods and sea. This was the old manor house of Porlock, with a history going back to the days of William the Conqueror, who gave it to Baldwin of Exeter. At Ashley Combe a toll road climbs up through woodlands in a series of bends to join the main A.39 at Culbone Stables.

Porlock Weir is a place of quiet beauty, with ancient cottages, inn and harbour, looking out across the sweeping bay to Hurlstone Point and Selworthy Beacon. Savage, writing in 1830, says there were then many fishing boats in the harbour, primarily engaged

during the herring season, and three trading sloops. Trade declined
with the coming of the railways, though no rail ever reached Porlock,
and now only a few fishing boats use the tiny harbour, with some
yachts joining them for the summer months.

CULBONE

Today, Culbone consists of a tiny church, a progressive pottery
run by man and wife, and a cottage where teas are served. A description left by the Rev. Richard Warner, who visited it in 1799, portrays
it exactly:

'In the centre of the little recess stands the Lilliputian church of Culbone, a
Gothic structure, 33 feet in length and 12 in breadth, with a cemetery of propor-
tionate dimensions and the remnants of an ancient stone-cross. Two cottages
planted just without the consecrated ground, are its only companions in this
secluded dell.'

A plate in his little book reveals that the church was then without
a spire. In the Domesday Book and until about 1750, it was known
as Kitnore, 'a hiding place by the sea', but after this time it gradually
assumed the name of Culbone, from the saint to whom the church is
dedicated. Bark strippers, the oak bark was used in tanning, and
charcoal burners, worked in the surrounding woods up to the
middle of the 19th century; while smuggled goods were landed on the
perilous beach 600 feet below. Outwardly Culbone has changed but
little in its long history. It is usually approached along a woodland
path from above Porlock Weir. The distance is about two miles,
and except for one or two stiff, sharp climbs which can be slippery
in wet weather, it is a pleasant walk with occasional glimpses of the
sea.

COUNTY GATE AND GLENTHORNE

Seven miles west of Porlock the road passes out of Somerset
and into Devon at County Gate. A hundred years ago it was known
as Cosgates-Feet, and a gate was hung across the road. From the
car park here there is a fine view up to Oare and down the East
Lyn valley towards Brendon. Probably the greatest feat this road
has witnessed was the dragging of the Lynmouth lifeboat up Countisbury Hill and down to Porlock Weir on the night of 12th January,
1899. A ship of 2,000 tons, the *Forrest Hall*, had lost her rudder and
was drifting on to the rocks. A raging sea prevented the launch of
the lifeboat at her home station. Undaunted, the crew and helpers
conveyed the boat over the narrow, exposed moorland road, 1,400
feet high in places, removing gateposts, digging out corners, and
knocking down a few cottage walls in Porlock. A launch was suc-
cessfully made at Porlock Weir, and the lifeboat stood by the vessel
until it was safely towed across to Wales.

Almost opposite County Gate is the way down to Glenthorne
where the Halliday family has lived for nearly 200 years. For a

Culbone Church.

small charge visitors can follow a Nature Trail down to the beach, a walk of nearly three miles, and descending 1,000 feet. Half-a-mile further along the main road and towards the sea is Old Barrow Hill, the site of a small Roman fort.

FORELAND POINT AND COUNTISBURY

From just above the church at Countisbury, a path leads out two miles to the lighthouse on the tip of Foreland Point. It is a bleak, wild headland, jutting into the Bristol Channel, the haunt of gulls, cormorants and jackdaws. In December 1971 the National Trust announced their acquisition of 705 acres of land on the Point. The church holds little of interest, except that the local folk seemed to have pulled it down and rebuilt it themselves a number of times in the last century. A relic of the old coaching days is the village inn, the Blue Ball, where two of the six horses were taken off after the climb up Countisbury Hill.

Just below some old cottages on the main road, and at the large Countisbury Hill warning sign, a bridle path leads up to an Iron Age fort built high on a ridge between the sea and the valley of the East Lyn.

The superb Exmoor coastal scenery reaches a climax around Lynton. Here the cliffs become even more precipitous, the dark gorge of the Lyn strikes deep into the hillside, and the spectacular Valley of the Rocks lies cradled high above the sea. Lynton, set on an uneven plain 500 feet above Lynmouth, is a small Victorian town with all the needful shops, hotels, and guest houses. An old cottage houses the Lyn and Exmoor Museum, which has a wide collection of local bye-gones. From the churchyard, thoughtfully provided with seats, there is a magnificent view up to Countisbury Hill and the Forelands.

Lynmouth is more picturesque, though it can often be over-crowded in August. Beneath overhanging rocks and trees, a narrow street runs nearly parallel to the river in the direction of the harbour. It is all a gay medley of fuchias, roses, colour-washed cottages, tiny, bright shops, and the continual song of the Lyn on its way to the sea. The cliff railway, first opened in 1890, and operated by gravity adjusted by water ballast, links the two villages.

VALLEY OF THE ROCKS

At Lynmouth the main A.39 turns inland to Blackmoor Gate and Barnstaple, following the lovely valley of the East Lyn for the first three miles. Westwards, the remaining coastal hamlets of the National Park are served by quiet byways, and the rolling landscape imparts a feeling of rural isolation. A mile beyond Lynton is the Valley of the Rocks, where the rocks have weathered through the centuries into strange forms. Some have been given names like the 'Castle Rock', 'Devil's Cheesewring', and the 'White Lady'. There is a spectacular cliff path to the Valley from Lynton by the North Walk, and a good description of the place is found in *Lorna Doone* when John Ridd visits Mother Meldrum in her winter abode within the Devil's Cheesewring. Hazlitt, who spent a few days at Lynton with Coleridge in the early years of the 19th century, tells in his *My First Acquaintance with the Poets:*

'At Linton the character of the sea-coast becomes more marked and rugged. There is a place called the Valley of the Rocks bedded among precipices over-hanging the sea, with rocky caverns beneath, into which the waves dash, and where the sea-gull forever wheels its screaming flight. A thunder-storm came on while we were at the inn, and Coleridge was running out bare-headed to enjoy the commotion of the elements in the Valley of the Rocks, but as if in spite, the clouds only muttered a few angry sounds, and let fall a few refreshing drops. Coleridge told me that he and Wordsworth were to have made this place the scene of a prose-tale, which was to have been in the manner of, but far superior to the *Death of Abel*, but they had relinquished the design.'

LEE ABBEY AND WOODY BAY TO COMBE MARTIN

This stretch of the coastal road is narrow and twisting all the way to Combe Martin, and near Lee Abbey there is a section of toll road. Lee Abbey, as it has been called since 1841, stands in an estate of 260 acres, and is a Conference Centre catering especially for young folk, combined with a Hotel open throughout the year. Originally it was known as Ley Manor, with Hugh Wichehalse as the squire of Lynton, and as such they appear in *Lorna Doone*.

At Woody Bay the steep slopes around the mile-wide bay are thickly covered in oaks, with a handful of dwellings set among them. As the road winds through the trees there are glimpses of the sea and rocks far below until it turns inland to Martinhoe. By the side of the neat church, parts of which are 11th century, a track leads down to The Beacon, a Roman fort that replaced the one on Old Barrow, near County Gate. Through many a bend the way goes on to Hunter's Inn, invitingly set among the trees, and here a mile long footpath follows the river Heddon to its outlet into the sea. Depending on the weather, Heddon's Mouth can either be a delightful glen, or a place of fury in a northerly gale, a veritable 'hell's mouth' as its name implies. Isolated, rock strewn, and inhospitable as the beach is, a deserted lime kiln shows that vessels once brought limestone here from Wales.

An even narrower road, grass grown down the middle, goes off to Trentishoe, a hamlet of church, farmhouse, and two or three cottages. There are fine views of the rocky coast and sea from Trentishoe Down, before the road crosses the edge of Holdstone Down (1,145 feet) to Stony Corner and down into Combe Martin on the north-western edge of the National Park.

Brendon Hills

These hills form the eastern part of the National Park, and are cut off from the rest by the deep valleys of the rivers Exe and Avill. Only at Wheddon Cross is the gap bridged, and here an arm of the Brendons reaches out to grasp a shoulder of Dunkery. Villages and hamlets of long existence lie scattered among the foothills; Withycombe, Rodhuish, Roadwater to the north; Monksilver on the extreme eastern edge; Elworthy and Brompton Regis to the south; Exton, Cutcombe, and Timberscombe down the western boundary, formed by the Dulverton—Dunster road. Amid the central hills are Luxborough and Treborough, and the scattered hamlet of Withiel Florey. A brief account of all these villages will be found in the Gazetteer.

WOODLAND AND GRASSLAND

Extensive conifer plantations between Dunster and Luxborough belong to the Forestry Commission, and cover much of Croydon Hill. Fortunately, some of the hill tops have been left as open heath, so the regiments of trees do not completely dominate the skyline. A wooded valley with mixed trees and streams running down through Druid's Combe to Roadwater, and the narrow, twisting road to Comberow, are among the most lovely parts of the Brendons.

To these can be added the broad-leaved woodlands of the river Haddeo, and the open ridge road from Elworthy to Wheddon Cross, never below 1,100 feet and with wide views over the hills and coastal plain to the Bristol Channel and Wales. Raleigh's Cross inn on this route has long been a landmark for travellers and others—a welcome sight to packhorsemen escorting their loads along this crest to Exford, Challacombe and Barnstaple; to drovers with their flocks passing down to the markets at Taunton, Bampton and Tiverton; to miners emerging into the light from the bowels of these Brendon Hills; and still gladly spied by the tourists of today passing on to the wilder places of Exmoor.

Almost all the farmland around is given over to grazing for sheep and cattle, except between Roadwater and Monksilver, where the ground drops below 500 feet and some corn is grown. A mile east of Wheddon Cross is Heath Poult Cross, a local name of the black grouse, a bird now very scarce on Exmoor. Close by is Lype Hill, 1,390 feet high, and the highest point in Somerset apart from the Exmoor hills.

MINING

All these hills have an attractive rural beauty, and here the roads and walks are seldom overcrowded. But they had a narrow escape in the last century when sustained attempts were made to mine copper and iron ore, and for which a railway was built from the port of Watchet to the top of Brendon Hill, and then along to Goosemoor. A mining community of 750 sprang up, and during the peak period from 1874-8, over 40,000 tons of ore were mined annually. Certainly, it was fortunate for the landscape of the region that by the early 1880s cheaper ore was found elsewhere, and mining on the Brendons came to a halt. All that now remains is the bed of the railway, including the steep 1 in 4 incline at Comberow, a multitude of shafts (most of them sealed or fenced), and some ruined buildings just west of Raleigh's Cross. Perhaps the only enduring results are two Methodist Chapels at Gupworthy and Beulah built for the miners, and still used for a regular Sunday service. The small congregation now comes from the farming community around, but Beulah Terrace, once occupied by mining families, is derelict and fast disappearing.

There are many lovely spots among the Brendon Hills, and they are well worth discovering. Excellent walks start from the pack-horse bridge at Dunster and on to Carhampton, Withycombe, Timberscombe, or Luxborough. Many woodland paths are open to ramblers, and a motor road passes through the forest on Croydon Hill, which has a pleasant car park and picnic area.

3 Man and the Moor

Early Times

Man has lived on Exmoor for several thousand years, but the population only began to make headway once the climate had started to improve after about 2000 B.C. We know this from the variety and quantity of monuments dating from the so-called Beaker Period and the Bronze Age, the latter lasting until c.500 B.C., when it faded into the Iron Age. These monuments consist mainly of barrows, stone circles and standing stones, located on hill tops and on other high ground over the Moor.

Most of the barrows are constructed of turf and stones, often 30 feet long and up to 9 feet high, and were originally the burial places of local chieftains. Very little is known about these early settlers, but they must have been a pastoral people, keeping sheep and cattle, and taking refuge among the moorland wastes in times of trouble. The Five Barrows group on the Somerset—Devon border south-west of Simonsbath, and Chapman Barrows above Challacombe, are fine examples. The most accessible are the two Rowbarrows (1,674 feet), about a mile west of Dunkery Beacon; Alderman's Barrow (1,466 feet) on the left-hand side of the westerly Lucott—Exford road, the Wembarrows (1,404 feet) on the crown of Winsford Hill; and the Five Barrows (1,618 feet) near Kinsford Gate, mentioned above. These, and many others, are all clearly marked on the 1-inch Ordnance Survey map, and are described in Charles Whybrow's Microstudy, *Antiquary's Exmoor*.

Stone circles are not easy to find, especially after the bracken has grown up at the end of June. One on Withypool Hill contains about thirty stones; another just off the Porlock—Exford road at Colley Water has about twenty. Some of the isolated stones set up on the moorland are only 19th century boundary stones, or rubbing stones for cattle. But many are ancient, and the most notable is the Longstone, $9\frac{1}{2}$ feet high, a mile east of Chapman Barrows. It may have been meant as a marker or guide post, for this is a very bleak part of the moor, but more likely it is a memorial stone to a Bronze Age ruler. The Longstone is best approached from the gateway 200 yards west of the Somerset-Devon border on the Simonsbath—Challacombe road, B.3358.

Iron Age inhabitants of Exmoor, living between the Bronze Age and the Roman occupation in the first century A.D., left behind some twenty earthworks or 'castles', often of striking shape and size. The largest is on top of Countisbury Hill, just west of the village, a linear fortification with a high rampart and a deep ditch on its east side. Another is Shoulsbarrow (Shoulsbury) Castle, a rectangular fort enclosing about five acres, west of the highest point on the

Challacombe—High Bray road. A third is Cow Castle, perched on the summit of a steep hill, three miles below Simonsbath, at the junction of White Water and the river Barle. Another outstanding construction, which may belong either to this or to medieval times, is Tarr Steps: the mighty clapper causeway referred to later.

Romans, Saxons, Danes and Normans

Roman penetration of Exmoor was confined to the coast—to two signal stations already mentioned: the first at Old Barrow near County Gate, the second at Martinhoe; both designed to keep a watch on the Bristol Channel. A later link with this period is the Caratacus Stone on Winsford Hill, probably not erected until a hundred years or so after the Roman legions had left Britain in c. 410 A.D., and when the country was suffering a series of new invasions from the south and east. The Saxons took two hundred years to reach the West Country, and for a time were totally held up by a stout defence under the leadership of the semi-legendary Arthur. By the early 700s, however, the Saxons were in possession of Taunton, and thereafter drove the native British tribes south-west into Cornwall or north-west into Wales. They then proceeded to consolidate their conquest of Devon and Somerset and, so far as Exmoor was concerned, settled mainly in the valleys and low-lying areas outside the moorland proper. Here and there, however, they took over outlying native holdings, so that evidence of Saxon settlement is widespread, much of it vested in place names still with us, — *worthy* (Pinkworthy), *ton* or *tun* (Dulverton), *ham* (Cornham), and *cot* (Narracott), all of which mean a farm of some nature. Another indication is the small fields (now seen as orchards and lambing enclosures) next to the farmsteads, hemmed in by massive hedge-banks; also boundary ditches and sunken droves.

The Saxon occupation of the west did not continue undisturbed. In the 9th century Norse and Danish pirates began raiding all round the coast, and in the east they came to stay in what is now known as East Anglia. In Somerset, however, they had no success. The steep cliffs and scarcity of landing-places enabled the defenders to beat them off in a series of successful engagements, notably at Watchet in 919 and at Porlock in 989; while at Porlock again in 1052 the then outlawed Harold, future king of England, was repulsed by local forces. By this time Somerset and Devon had become distinct administrative units or shires sub-divided into hundreds, containing a well-developed pattern of farming, grouped about various manors, with pastures, ploughed fields, mills, and much common and waste land.

We have this information on the written authority of Domesday Book, the great inventory of property drawn up for William 1 in in 1086, twenty years after the Norman invasion and subsequent pacification of the country. The Normans conducted a take-over

Dunkery from Selworthy.

in the best contemporary sense. While retaining the Saxon pattern of settlement, they expelled almost all the Saxon lords and handed their estates to Norman knights who had rendered service to William. For example, William de Mohun, a close friend of the Conqueror, received not only Dunster but the land of 46 other manors. Ralf de Limesi was given East Luccombe; Porlock went to Baldwin of Exeter; and Timberscombe to Roger Arundel. Robert de Obdurville received estates in various parts of Somerset, and his Exmoor grants included the manors of Withypool, Hawkridge, and Exton. He was also appointed Baron of the Royal Forests of Somerset, and was almost certainly the first Warden of Exmoor, a post which remained in his family for 150 years.

The Royal Forest

While the reclamation of land all over Somerset and Devon continued apace under the feudal system maintained by the Normans— much of it in the form of enclosed holdings won out of the waste— large areas of unoccupied and virtually unused land remained: unused, that is, except for hunting. Exmoor was one such area. Saxon kings had probably first made it so, for apart from specific references in Domesday, we know of their general love of hunting and hawking, if only from such terms as *deer, stag, hind, hound, horn*, *slot*, and *harbourer*, all Saxon in origin. As in other matters, William seized on Exmoor and established it as a Royal Forest— the word *forest* meaning not 'trees' but land outside of normal agricultural use—and protected it by harsh legislation. Here the wild red deer were reserved for the king's pleasure, and those who killed them unlawfully suffered mutilation. Cruel laws, the damage done to crops by the deer, and the fluctuation of Forest boundaries (under King John, they extended as far east as the line of the river Exe), were a mounting source of grievance. Gradually, however, the Forest area contracted, so that by 1301 it coincided with little more than the present parish of Exmoor together with the parish of Oare. At the same time law enforcement was humanised.

Originally the Warden of Exmoor was a royal official, whose main task was to look after the pasturage and the deer, the 'king's vert and venison', maintain the boundaries, and generally protect the royal interests. He was paid an annual fee (£11.92 in 1289), chiefly obtained from charges for cattle and sheep grazing during the summer months. He and his officers were assisted by two classes of farmers, who enjoyed certain hereditary privileges connected with grazing, fishing, and the right to cut turf, heath and fern inside the Forest. These were the Free Suitors of Withypool and Hawkridge (52 tenement holders in those parishes, who had free access to the Forest as described), and the Suitors at Large (mainly representatives of the 'townships' and owners of land bordering the Forest, who paid half-rates for grazing). The Free Suitors had to take part in the regular round-ups of horses, cattle and sheep, perambulate the boundary every seven years, and serve on the coroner's jury. The latter had fewer duties, but both had to attend the Swainmote or Forest Court which investigated complaints and enforced regulations. The Swainmote normally met in a field close to Landacre Bridge on the morning after Ascension Day, and in Hawkridge churchyard on the morning of Friday of Pentecost. They usually adjourned to complete business at Withypool, either in the inn or at the pound. Sometime in the 17th century the Swainmote was moved to Simonsbath, and it was here that the last court was held in 1818.

In 1508 Henry VII decided to lease the Royal Forest to the Warden in return for an annual rent of £46.49. Providing that at least a hundred head should be in the Forest at the end of the lease, the deer ceased to be a royal prerogative; and the emphasis shifted from preserving animals of the chase to pasturing farm beasts on the moorland. Henceforward this became the main source of revenue available to the Warden. Each spring he sent his men into the local markets to 'cry the moor', i.e. announce the rates at which sheep and cattle could be sent into the Forest for grazing between March and October, ponies being allowed all the year round.

30,000 was a common total for sheep, ranging from 8p. per score in 1570 to 17p. in 1642, at which rate the charge remained unchanged until 1818. Far fewer cattle and ponies were involved, and rates for them ranged from 1p. to 3p. per head. While grazing was the most valuable asset of the Forest, every part of the moorland vegetation had its uses. Heather was gathered by broomsquires for making brushes, gorse fired bakehouse ovens, rushes were used for floor covering, bracken for stable litter, reeds for thatching. Nuts were harvested for food, charcoal burners plied their trade in many a hidden combe, and willows were used—as now—for baskets, panniers, cradles, and other containers.

The 17th Century

This was a time of trouble for Exmoor. During the Civil War, 1642-5, detachments of Royalists and Roundheads frequently travelled through the territory, though no major engagements were fought. The castles at Dunster and Ilfracombe were besieged, and in June 1645 Prince Charles (then 15 years old) stayed for a while at Dunster on his way to Barnstaple. Under the Commonwealth the Royal Forest, deemed to be a 'parcel of the possession of Charles Stewart, late King of England', came up for sale. A survey in 1651 assessed the area at 18,927 acres, with an annual value of £473, and provided a useful record of boundary marks. The surveyor, Jeremie Baines, was not very complimentary, stating:

'That the said Chase is mountainous and cold ground, much beclouded with thick fogges and mists, and is used for depasturing cattle, horses, sheep, and is a very sound sheep pasture. But a very great part thereof is overgrown with heath and yielding but a poor kind of turf of little value here'.

In 1652 the Royal Forest was sold for £6,857.72 to a certain James Boevey, a London merchant of Dutch extraction, a man of strange character and remarkable initiative. He picked on Simonsbath as a suitable centre, built a substantial house—still standing in the village today—and enclosed 100 acres for a home farm. This was the first house within the confines of the Forest and remained so until the 19th century. Boevey made himself felt in more ways than one, for during his forty years on Exmoor he started at least 17 legal actions against his neighbours. In particular he laid claim to various commons surrounding the Forest, and was only defeated after a five-year battle in the courts. With the restoration of the monarchy in 1660, all previous Crown lands reverted to Charles II on the simple grounds that the 'late usurping powers' had no right to sell another person's property. Boevey, however, was not to go, for although he lost the freehold of Exmoor, he had taken the precaution of buying a life interest in the lease, and remained Warden until his death in 1696.

Mention must here be made of the Doones for, as related in Chapter 4, there is historical evidence of their existence as a gang of rustlers, if nothing else. Blackmore's romance was based on traditional tales about them, and one theory has it that they arrived at the beginning of the 17th century and were expelled at the end of it. It is difficult to account for their co-existence, however, with Boevey (who never mentioned them); for although the 'Doone Valley' lay outside the Forest, it is hardly likely that either party would have kept the peace unless some private understanding had been reached. But of this there is no record.

The End of the Royal Forest

The Royal Forest continued to be leased throughout the 18th century, and in 1784 the Wardenship passed into the hands of the Acland family. In due course the Sir Thomas Acland of the day applied for an extension of the lease beyond the next expiry date in 1814. It was the period of the Napoleonic Wars, England had been thrown back on her own resources, and the Government was looking around for fresh supplies of naval timber. Exmoor seemed a possible place where trees might be grown, and a new survey was put in hand with this plan in mind. According to the report issued in June 1814, the acreage was somewhat larger than in Boevey's day, while the grazing of sheep and other animals returned over £400 p.a. to Sir Thomas. Mention was also made of 37 trees, mostly round Simonsbath, where Boevey's house was serving as an inn. The first proposal was to 'deforest' and enclose the entire area, make allocations of land to the interested landholders, and reserve 10,000 acres to the Crown for timber production. After the battle of Waterloo, however, strategic priorities changed, and in 1818 it was decided to sell the Crown allotment outright. The purchaser was John Knight, an ironmaster from the Midlands, who paid £50,000 or £5 an acre, and who went on to buy the Acland and certain other allotments as well. By 1820 he had acquired about 15,500 acres (some three-quarters of the old Royal Forest) and the farmstead of Simonsbath as well. Thus a thousand years of Exmoor history came to an end.

The Great Reclamation

The story of the Knights—John, and his son, Frederic—spans the 19th century; and the reader is recommended to read the full account in C. S. Orwin's classic, *The Reclamation of Exmoor Forest*, as revised and extended by Roger Sellick in the edition published in 1970. Suffice it to say here that the enterprise fell into three main categories. On the land, an initial period of intensive effort and investment by John to convert the uplands into mixed arable and stock husbandry broke down. This policy was abandoned after 1841 by Frederic, who carved out separate farmsteads at Honeymead,

Cornham, Emmetts Grange, and eight other places, attracted tenants on favourable terms, and encouraged them to improve the moorland by means of subsoiling and by grass and root rotations for the benefit of stock, mainly sheep. This plan paid off in the end, and in essence it represents the way Exmoor is hill farmed today. The Knights buttressed this basic economy with extensive road building, bank construction, hedge and tree planting, and all-round improvements to the estate. The second category was mining, whereby Frederic leased rights to several companies (mainly to the Dowlais Iron Company) in order to exploit the deposits of copper and iron ore known to exist, not only in the Royal Forest, but also in other parts of Exmoor—notably in the Brendons where mining was vigorously prosecuted between 1852-3 and 1882-3. The Knights were industrialists, but Frederic's instinct in this instance proved wrong. Although he urged the prospectors on, and started laying a mineral railway to carry the ore from Simonsbath to the port of Porlock Weir, none of the mining was profitable and in the end the whole enterprise had to be abandoned. It may be said—a fortunate result for Exmoor. The last category concerned people. Thanks to the employment provided by the estate, the recognition of a new parish of Exmoor centred on Simonsbath, and the building of a church, school, inn, and various dwellings both in the village and outside, the old Royal Forest was supporting as many as 300 people by the 1880s, without having lost its innate character as a wild upland, partly harmonised by man.

Robbers' Bridge, Oare Valley

Exmoor in the 20th Century

After the untimely death of his son, Frederic Knight sold the reversion of the estate to the Fortescue family, his neighbours at Filleigh, and who entered into possession in 1897. No essential change was made in that the two estates were integrated, and farm practice balanced by summering many of the cattle and sheep on the moorland, and by wintering and finishing them in the vale. Since a large part of Exmoor as a whole was in the hands of big landowners, this remained the pattern in the first third of the present century, owners and occupiers alike weathering as best they could the bad times that afflicted British agriculture between the 1880s and the 1940s. 1927 saw the start of the break-up of the Fortescue-Knight holding, when four farms were sold to Sir Robert Waley Cohen; and the process continued after the war when further farms were sold away. In 1969 Somerset County Council bought 2,000 acres near Simonsbath, comprising Driver and Pinkworthy Farms, and The Chains.

The Second World War, and the legislation that followed it, brought help to farmers generally and to Exmoor farmers in particular—through guaranteed prices and capital and other grants. Without such aid, the agricultural economy of the Moor would not survive. But changes were not confined to farming. In the National Parks Act 1949 the idea took shape that certain regions of the country deserved protection, for their wild life, natural beauty, and historical interest—providing access for all who wished to respect and enjoy these amenities, as part of the national heritage. It was this Act that enabled Exmoor to become a National Park in 1954. But it was not the start of the story, for protection was already in being in those parts of Exmoor controlled or owned by the National Trust, best described as 'a private organisation with public responsibility'. The process had begun in 1918 when the Acland family leased nearly 1,300 acres of moorland on Winsford Hill and Tarr Steps. In 1932 Colonel W. Wiggin gave 860 acres, including the summit of Dunkery Beacon, while Mrs. Allan Hughes added a further 945 acres in 1934. In 1944 Sir Richard Acland handed over the Holnicote Estate, nearly 10,000 acres, including most of the villages of Selworthy, Bossington, Allerford, Luccombe, and five hamlets besides. Holnicote House is now leased to the Holiday Fellowship. Sections of the Lyn Valley have also been acquired by the Trust, likewise land at Heddon's Mouth, Trentishoe Down and Woody Bay. The most recent purchase concerns 705 acres at Foreland Point, Countisbury, made in December 1971.

The Public and Exmoor

The status of Exmoor as a National Park, and its increasing popularity with tourists, has generated a number of problems. The central difficulty is to combine the visitors' natural desire to enjoy the Moor on foot, on horseback, or in a car, with the legitimate use of the available land for farming and forestry; and at the same time to resist all such pressures so that the natural character and life of Exmoor, as a recognised region, can continue. Too many cars clog the roads and the villages, too many feet erode the paths, careless people damage property, over-active farmers want here and there to plough up moorland and enclose it with fencing, foresters want to plant many more trees, usually conifers. The Exmoor Society was actually founded in 1958 to combat a plan by the Forestry Commission to plant up The Chains. It has since acted partly as a watchdog—in the main, resisting plough-up and enclosure—and partly as a source of constructive ideas for the use of the Park. A recent plan was the 'Greenway', which proposed that the railway track between Taunton and East Anstey, and possibly that between Taunton and Minehead as well, be converted into an amenity route for horsemen, cyclists, ramblers and naturalists, adapting certain stations as picnic and recreation centres in order to siphon off some of the day-visitors before they enter the narrow moorland roads. The National Park Authorities have turned down this proposal in the main, but it is possible that a portion of it may be salved—particularly in view of the plans for opening up access to Exmoor, consequent upon the construction of the M5 Motorway and the feeder routes that will follow.

The future of Exmoor lies in wise planning, and in adjusting the interests of those who live on and by the Moor, and of those who rely on it for refreshment through Nature.

4 'Lorna Doone' and other Literary Associations

The romance of *Lorna Doone* by R. D. Blackmore is related by 'I, John Ridd, of the parish of Oare in the county of Somerset'. The wild Doones had killed his father when returning from Porlock market. In addition to this and other crimes, they had kidnapped Lorna when a child. John accidently meets her in the Badgworthy valley, falls in love, and eventually joins up with the local people to rid Exmoor of the plundering, murdering, Doones. The book contains some wonderful descriptions of the Moor, its rivers, combes, uplands, and changing seasons, together with various local legends and historical events. Included is an account of the battle of Sedgemoor of 1685, and this sets the story as taking place in the latter half of the 17th century.

Of the whole of Exmoor we can truly say, 'Here is the land of the Doones'. From Dulverton to Combe Martin, from South Molton to Lynton, all this country is included in the story of *Lorna Doone*. John Ridd spent a night at Dunster; John Fry rightly described Dunkery Beacon as 'The haighest place on Hexmoor'; Tom Faggus sought refuge in the Ship Inn, Porlock; the outlaws had their lair near Badgworthy Water; while Lorna was married in Oare Church.

The Doone Valley

Malmsmead, shown as Moles Mead on an old map, midway between Oare and Brendon, is the most convenient starting-point for a visit to Badgworthy Water and Hoccombe Combe, or the Doone Valley to give it its popular name. The National Park Authority has recently opened a large car park and picnic area at Malmsmead, and there are facilities for camping and teas. Apart from a few damp spots after wet weather, the walk up Badgworthy Water is quite easy with a well defined path all the way to the Doone Valley. This famous stream, flowing along its rocky channel and frequently cascading over miniature waterfalls, forms the boundary between Somerset and Devon. You start walking by the side of some farm buildings, pass through a couple of narrow meadows, and then up a short rise opposite Cloud Farm with its background of old Pines. Here is a fine view up Badgworthy, the water flanked by rowan, ash, and oleanders, and in the distance an ancient oak wood on the Devon side facing a Somerset plantation of firs. In the oak wood are grey squirrels and green woodpeckers; and while the red deer may not be seen, many harbour in the district.

The Barle above Simonsbath. Cornham on skyline.

Challacombe in winter.

Red Deer—Stag and Hinds—on Molland Moor.

(Colin Thornton)

Exmoor Mare at Landacre

(John Keene)

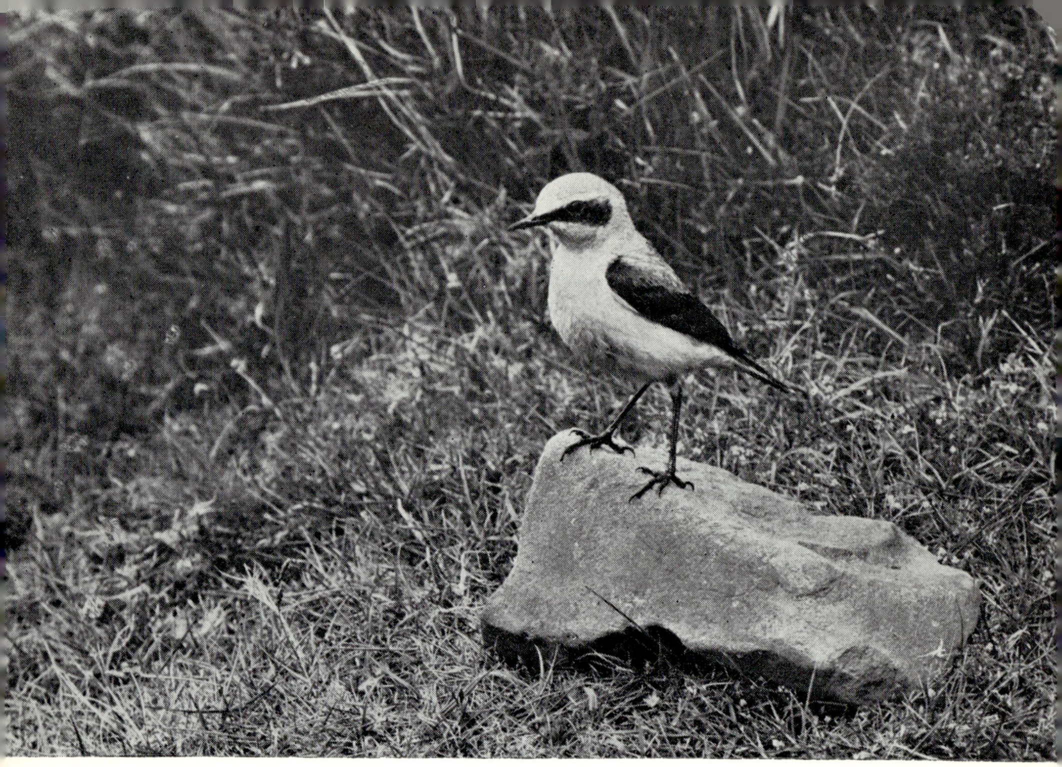

Wheatear.

Water-wheel housing at the Bampfylde Copper Mine, Heasley Mill.

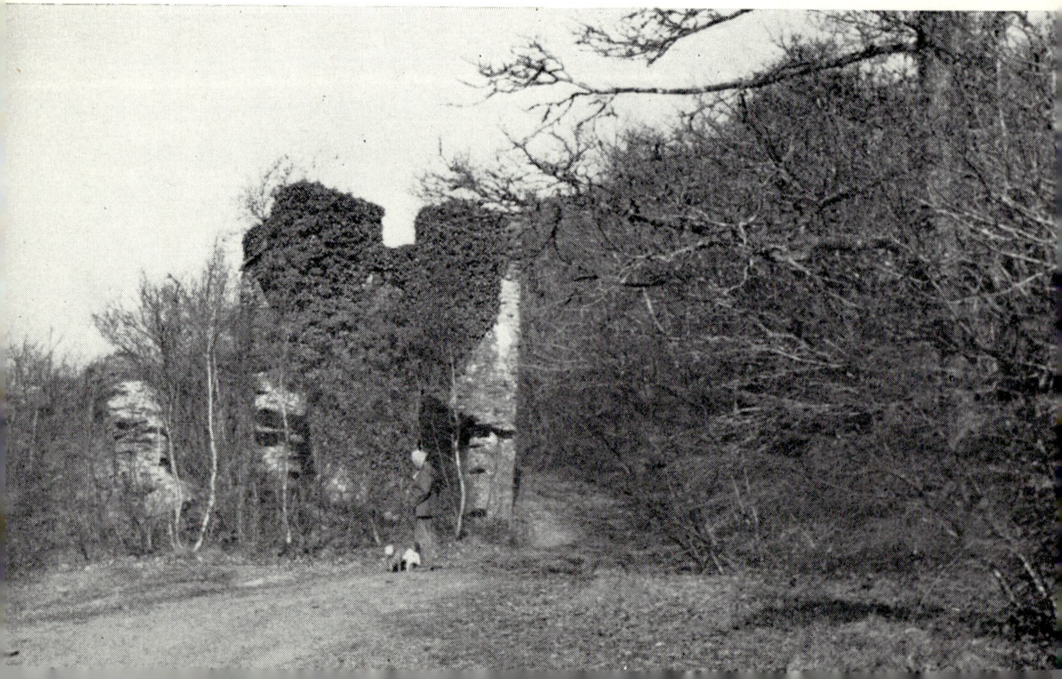

Just before the oaks are reached, and about half-way to Doone Valley, a plaque fixed to a great slab of rock commemorates R. D. Blackmore and *Lorna Doone*. No doubt, many folk on reaching this spot are convinced they have arrived at the site of the Doone settlement, and return well satisfied with their trip. But the medieval hamlet of Badgworthy was a mile further on, where the path rises above the stream and turns slightly away from it. Ahead is a thick row of beech trees, and a large bracken covered mound which guards the entrance to Hoccombe Combe, the Valley of the Doones.

This combe runs almost due west to its headwaters on Brendon Common, and though the sides are not steep, the valley is wide and has attractive grass swards on either side of the stream. Traces have been found of a building, probably a look-out, on top of the entrance mound, and down below on almost level ground the foundations of 14 cottages. It is now very difficult to find evidence of these buildings amid the bracken, ant hills and rabbit burrows. Further on, a large pile of rubble marks the site of a cottage occupied by a Fortescue shepherd, Jack Jones, until 1940. He lived here with his wife and daughter before the Army took over the area for training purposes, and they had to be evacuated by horse and cart to Simonsbath. However, the evidence is clear that this was the site of an early settlement, at least until the middle of the 15th century; and that if the Doones ever lived on Exmoor, here was their stronghold.

Fact or Fiction?

Whether the Doones ever existed as a marauding band is not easily resolved, but certainly they were not entirely the product of Blackmore's vivid imagination. Murray's *Handbook for Travellers in Devon and Cornwall* of 1859 (ten years before *Lorna Doone* was published) had this account of them:

'One mile left of the double gates [Brendon Two Gates], in a bottom called the Warren, are some remains of a building which was once the stronghold of the Doones of Badgworthy, a daring gang of robbers who infested the borders of the moor at the time of the Commonwealth, and of whom the tradition is still extant. They are said to have been natives of another part of England, and to have entered Devonshire about the time of Cromwell's usurpation. It is certain that for many years they were a terror to the neighbourhood of Lynton, and long succeeded in levying blackmail on the farmers, and in escaping with their booty to this lonely retreat, where none dare follow. At length, however, they committed so savage a murder that the whole country was aroused, and a large party of the peasantry, having armed themselves, proceeded at once to Badgworthy, and captured the entire gang. This exploit ended the career of the Doones, for they were shortly afterwards tried for their numerous crimes and deservedly executed.'

Dr. Collyns in his famous work, *The Chase of the Wild Red Deer*, states on page 114 of the first edition, 1862, 'In a wild combe may still be seen the remains of some buildings once the stronghold of the Doones of Badgworthy'. The Rev. J. F. Chanter possessed a manuscript book of West Country legends prepared for his father in 1839, and which included *Legends of the Doones of Badgworthy*. So it is clear beyond dispute that the Doones were known long before the publication of Blackmore's novel in 1869.

Origin of the Doones

Various ideas have been put forward. Among the most likely are:

1. They have been confused through the mists of time with the Danes, who once plundered along the northern coast of Devon and Somerset.

2. They were members of a Welsh clan, the Dwn, and which is pronounced 'Doon'. It is known that some of its members fled from Carmarthen across the Bristol Channel to England.

3. The Rev. W. H. P. Greswell suggests in his book, *The Forests and Deer Parks of the County of Somerset* 1905:

'In the summer of 1645, Goring's troopers, a rascally crew, were overrunning North Devon, possibly Exmoor, and if the Doone robbers really lived in the Doone Valley, they might well have been recruited by waifs and strays of this disorganised force.'

Goring was a royalist commander in the civil war, who was defeated at Langport and escaped abroad to Spain. An entry in the church book for Minehead, 1645, reads, 'Lost of the church stocke beinge plundered when Lord Goringe was heere'.

Malmsmead.

4. After the battle of Sedgemoor, 6 July 1685, many West Country men went into hiding, and no doubt some of them sought refuge in the wild wasteland of Exmoor, and were driven to desperate acts in order to survive.

5. Strange as it may seem, the weight of the evidence suggests that the gang had a Scottish origin, and accompanied a nobleman named Ensor Doune when he was expelled from Scotland in the first half of the 17th century. After about 70 years, by which time some of the men were involved in plundering, they all returned to their homeland. The main support for this theory was given in a long letter written by 'Audrie Doon' (Ida M. Browne), and printed in the *West Somerset Free Press* of 12 October 1901.

R. D. Blackmore

R. D. Blackmore was born in 1825, and after 1858 lived mainly at Teddington, Middlesex, where he died in 1900. Before settling at Teddington he spent many years around Exmoor when his father was curate at Culmstock, and then at Ashford, near Barnstaple. These two places are woven into his novels, *Perlycross* and *The Maid of Sker*. Other members of his family had long been established in the moorland parish of Parracombe, while his grandfather was vicar of Oare for over thirty years until his death in 1842. As a youth the future novelist spent many holidays with these Exmoor relatives, exploring the countryside which was to form the background of his famous story, and hearing tales of the Doones. After the plan for writing *Lorna Doone* had been conceived, Blackmore spent some weeks at Withypool, where a part of the work was written in the Royal Oak inn. Without doubt the wide notoriety of the Doones is due almost entirely to Blackmore's romance, first published in 1869. The book came out in three volumes, a common practice then, and sold only slowly, for the first edition was not exhausted until 1872. In the preface to the 20th edition, Blackmore tells how popular success came to his book. Princess Louise, daughter of Queen Victoria, became through marriage in 1871 the Marchioness of Lorne, and somehow in the public mind she came to be associated with the story. Once the book was generally known, it soon gained popularity; and over the past 100 years it has remained continually in print. It has also been filmed several times.

Other Literary Associations

Towards the close of the 18th century Coleridge and his friends made several excursions into Exmoor. He was then living in the Quantock village of Nether Stowey, with Wordsworth and his sister Dorothy some two miles away at Alfoxden. In the autumn of 1797 they journeyed together along the coast to Lynton and the Valley of the Rocks, and during this walk they jointly planned

Coleridge's most famous poem, *The Rhyme of the Ancient Mariner*. In the following year Coleridge made the journey to Lynton again, when with Hazlitt, they passed by Dunster and Minehead, and tramped for 'miles on dark-brown heaths overlooking the Channel, with the Welsh hills beyond', until they finally reached Lynton after midnight. For breakfast they had tea, toast, eggs and honey, and found a copy of Thomson's *Seasons* lying on a window-seat, which caused Coleridge to exclaim, 'That is true fame'.

On a subsequent visit Coleridge walked down to Porlock Weir, up through the autumn tinted woods to Culbone, and stayed at a farm-house usually identified with Ash Farm, about a quarter of a mile beyond. Falling asleep in his chair one afternoon, he dreamed the incidents of his fragmentary poem, *Kubla Khan*. Awakening, he began to write down the impressions still clear in his mind, when he was interrupted by a caller from Porlock. An hour later when free again, he found the remaining lines had slipped from his memory and were forever lost.

For a time in 1799 Robert Southey, the poet-laureate, lived in Minehead and left a brief account of the town. On a wet afternoon he was detained for some hours in the Ship Inn at Porlock, and wrote a sonnet to pass away the time. Shelley also stayed at Lynmouth from June to August 1807, and a 'Shelley' cottage is still pointed out. He spent his time writing pamphlets, many of them seditious, and it was here that he completed his long poem *Queen Mab*.

The first and best book on stag hunting, came from the pen of Dr. Charles Collyns, of Dulverton, in 1862, and his *Chase of the Wild Red Deer* is a classic on the subject. Sir John Fortescue's *Story of a Red Deer* has been reprinted many times; while Whyte-Melville's *Katerfelto* tells the story of an Exmoor pony, and includes a fine description of the turning tide in Porlock Bay. Probably the best Exmoor poem is Henry Newbolt's *A Song of Exmoor* which is included in his collected poems. Walter Raymond, who wrote many little books and articles on Somerset life, lived in a cottage at Withypool from 1905-14 which he rented for 5p. a week. The taking of the little cottage and his early days there, are described in his *Book of Simple Delights*.

Two nature writers whose works are still in considerable demand are Richard Jefferies and W. H. Hudson. Jefferies gathered material for his *Red Deer* around Dulverton, and an essay in his *Field and Hedgerow* tells of a visit to Selworthy. From 1923 until his death in 1950, E. W. Hendy lived in Bossington Lane, Porlock, and all his books contain fine accounts of Exmoor's wild life.

Many interesting books about Exmoor have been written by local authors. See the Bibliography in *The Exmoor Review* 1972.

5 Wild Life

Red Deer

Exmoor is the English stronghold of the wild Red Deer, *Cervus Elaphus*. Apart from much smaller numbers on the nearby Quantocks, and in the Lake District, resident herds are not to be found elsewhere in England. They disappeared from Dartmoor as long ago as 1780, and the only ones seen there today are wanderers from Exmoor.

The Red Deer of Exmoor are indigenous—native to the land—and those that roam the combes and moors today are completely wild and free. They are largely concentrated in wooded areas, with the main herds around Hawkcombe and Cloutsham, West Porlock and Culbone, the Quarme and Haddeo valleys, the Barle valley between Withypool and Dulverton, Grabbist woods above Dunster, and on the Brendons. Smaller herds may be met almost anywhere in the National Park. Except for the mating months of October and November the sexes live separately, the hinds and young in small herds of up to twenty, the stags in little groups of two or three, sometimes even solitary. The total numbers about 600 beasts.

TERMS, SIZE, COLOUR, FOOD

The correct descriptive terms for Red Deer are stag, hind, calf—not buck, doe, fawn. The last three terms apply to the smaller Fallow Deer which rarely occur on Exmoor outside the Brendons. Antlers or horns are carried only by the stag, and are usually referred to as the 'head'. An average stag stands some 3 feet 8 inches at the shoulder, the hind 3 feet 2 inches, and weigh about 12 and 10 stones respectively. It is the largest of all British wild animals. During the summer months the colouring is a reddish brown, but this becomes darker in the stag during the winter, and greyer in the hind.

Red Deer are largely woodland creatures, feeding during the night, and returning to their coverts at dawn. Throughout the spring and summer months they find sufficient food to their liking on the nearby heather moors, and in the woods around. Grass, tender leaves of saplings, bramble shoots, plants, young bracken and ivy, are all eaten. In the colder months they raid farmlands for root crops and young corn, and it is then that a herd can do a lot of damage in a single night.

The yearly shedding or mewing of the antlers is a remarkable phenomenon. They usually fall off in late March or April, and very occasionally a pair may be found close together on the moor. Almost immediately the replacement horns start to grow, forming at first a soft gristle-like substance, covered by a grey skin known as 'velvet'. By August the process is completed, the new horns have hardened, and the protective 'velvet' rubbed off against some sapling or branch.

October and November is the mating or rutting season, when the belling or roaring of stags resounds in the combes. Herds are formed, usually of five to ten hinds, under a dominant stag. Contests between males are frequent, but very rarely is one killed. Almost all the young are born or dropped among heather, bracken, or young woodland undergrowth, during June. The new-born calf is about the size of a hare, dapple-marked which fades away as the first winter coat grows. In the daytime the hind often remains concealed in a nearby wood, and only ventures out at nightfall to suckle the calf. Twins are extremely rare, and have never been satisfactorily proved. In the early weeks the main hazard is foxes, who may attack the young calf in the absence of its mother. Five or six months after birth the calf is able to fend for itself, though it may remain with its mother for almost another year.

In its second year the male will grow short knobs of horn, and in the third year the main horn or beam developes with one branch near the bottom called the 'brow'. Every year the antlers become stronger and larger with additional branches, the 'bay' and the 'trey', growing out of the main beam, and 'points' growing on the top of each antler. By the fifth year the normal stag will have on the main beam of each horn, counting from the bottom upwards, 'brow', 'bay', 'trey', plus two 'points' branching out at the top. At this stage it is considered to be an adult stag, but extra 'points' will grow on the top for a number of years, and the Exmoor record is 20. With the onset of old age the antlers no longer develop, and begin to 'go back' or deteriorate.

At 15 the animal is getting old, but individuals may live up to 20 years. It is when the teeth become loose and decayed that the deer's days are numbered, for then it cannot gather sufficient food in the hard winter months. However, this sad state of affairs is rarely reached on Exmoor where hunting culls the older and weaker animals.

SEEING THE RED DEER

Dusk is often the best time for seeing the deer when they move out of their woodland coverts to feed. But they may also be spotted feeding in young woodland at almost any hour. During the mating

Porlock Bay towards Hurlstone Point.

season in October and November there is much more daylight movement across the open moors, and also, of course, when they are being hunted. Borders of large woods, especially those which abut on to open moorland, e.g. above Cloutsham, on the north side of Winsford Hill, or on the top of Grabbist above Minehead— these are usually rewarding places. Summer growth of bracken and fern often shield them from view, and the russet autumn colours are a good camouflage. Deer rarely appear frightened of humans, but when surprised close at hand they move off at a fast trot. When they spot anyone at a distance, they will stand and stare for a few moments before moving slowly away. Stags may be unpredictable in the rutting season, and it is best to give them a wide berth, though there is no record of them ever attacking anyone on Exmoor.

See E. R. Lloyd's Microstudy, *The Wild Red Deer of Exmoor.*

Exmoor Pony

Among the farm animals to be seen on the moors and commons are small parties of Exmoor ponies. In 1819 Sir Thomas Acland drove the ponies off the old Royal Forest, and their descendants today form the pure bred herds running on Winsford Hill and Ashway side. Numbers were never very high, and the Moor has never been over-populated; indeed, the ponies were sadly depleted during the Second World War. In 1946 only six pure bred filly foals were born, but since then numbers have slowly increased. Now there are three pure bred, and three cross bred herds on Exmoor, and about forty others in various parts of the country.

The Exmoor Pony is a very ancient breed, and resembles the little horses of eastern Europe and Asia of 3,000 years ago more than any other breed in Britain. Together with the Red Deer, these ponies have roamed the high moorlands of Exmoor for thousands of years, probably before the arrival of any human inhabitants. Even now those on the open moors still remain but half-tame, and with the urge to wander they frequently break bounds. Terms used for ponies from the foal and onwards are: sucker, filly and colt; mare and stallion, and a working male is a gelding.

Distinctive features of the pure bred Exmoor Pony are the general brown colour ranging from red-brown (bay) to dark brown, lighter on flanks and underparts; the mealy coloured muzzle which is constant; bright 'toad' eyes and short pointed ears, and a complete absence of any white markings. A single white hair would exclude a pony from a pure bred herd. It is a small breed, stallions not above 12.3 hands, mares 12.2 at any age. If domesticated as suckers, most are admirably suitable for young folk and for trekking, but it needs an experienced rider to handle a mature pony straight off the moors. They are hardy little animals, well able to stand the hard winters of upland Exmoor, and make light work of the steep hillsides when used for shepherding. There is an annual gathering or round-up, and many cross bred ponies are offered for sale at Bampton Fair on the last Thursday of October. Pure breds are normally sold privately or through the Exmoor Pony Society. Herds of pure bred ponies can usually be seen on Codsend Moor, Ashway Side, and Winsford Hill, and cross breds on Withypool Common and Molland Moor.

In 1921 Reginald Le Bas, a Tiverton solicitor, founded the Exmoor Pony Society with Earl Fortescue as the first President. This Society, which now has branches in Canada, Denmark and the U.S.A., seeks to improve and encourage the breeding and registration of Exmoor Ponies, and maintains a Stud Book. Mrs. J. Watts, Quarry Cottage, Sampford Brett, near Williton, is the Secretary, and will be glad to supply additional information. Throughout the summer months ponies can be seen at Agricultural and Horse Shows in Somerset and Devon, but the main show is held at Exford in August.

See Anthony A. Dent's Microstudy, *The Pure Bred Exmoor Pony*.

Badger

Wooded and hilly country, with a stream not too far away, is the favourite haunt of the Badger, or Brock as it is affectionately known from the early Saxon name. As the skirts of Exmoor provide an abundance of this type of habitat, the Badger is quite a common animal. Being almost entirely nocturnal, few people realise there are hundreds of badgers in the National Park, and rarely see one unless it has been killed on the road, or caught in a snare. Sets or burrows are to be found in most of the older woods, and sometimes

Winsford.

in thick hedgerows with big trees, from the coast up to about 900 feet around Exford. The majority of Exmoor sets are built in banks, or on sloping ground, under rocky outcrops and beneath tree roots. Areas liable to flooding are always avoided, and the entrance holes are marked by great mounds of excavated earth. Some of the sets are very old, and badgers still live in the vicinity of the ancient hamlet of Brockwell, named after them, in the parish of Wootton Courtenay.

Badgers are omnivorous, for their diet consists of both flesh and vegetable food. Earthworms, snails, slugs, beetles, field mice, rats, hedgehogs, young rabbits, are all eaten, together with bulbs, especially bluebells, roots, plants, apples, potatoes, and blackberries. A special luxury, and one never passed by, is a wasps' nest, or better still that of the bee with lots of honey. Badgers often wander a mile or more in search of food, and sometimes may blunder into a hen-house. A housewife in the Brendons recently found a couple of badgers chasing her hens at midnight, but this rarely happens, and is certainly accidental.

The mating season is in late July and August, and the young are born in the following February and March. From the middle of April, the young, nearly always two to a family, appear above ground, and eventually accompany their parents on forages for food. Brock is a remarkably clean animal, and the bedding of leaves, moss, grass and bracken, is changed regularly. Unlike the fox, he never takes food (which may decay and smell) into the living quarters. He does not hibernate on Exmoor, but is much less active in winter than in summer. Longer periods are spent beneath ground asleep in a cosy nest, and he ventures out only twice or so a week in search of food.

Fox

Hunting has not diminished the number of foxes on Exmoor, and they are probably as abundant now as at any time in the past. They are quite widespread and occupy much the same type of country as the badger, although they are less restricted to wooded areas, and occur more frequently on the coastal cliffs. Except for the breeding season in late spring and summer, when the dog-fox and vixen share the family responsibilities, it is a solitary animal. While mainly nocturnal, it does wander about in the daytime, especially in isolated places, and when disturbed in the hunting season. The bark of the dog-fox at nights, a sharp 'yip-yip' which is sometimes repeated, and the scream of the vixen in January and February, are familiar Exmoor sounds.

On sunny days the fox may be surprised sleeping out in some quiet patch of bracken, gorse or heather, but invariably it leaps up before the walker is upon it, and makes off at a fast speed along some sheep track, glancing back at the intruder. The best chance of seeing foxes is to discover an earth or lair where the cubs play near the entrance, and are brought food by the parents. Around dawn and dusk from May to July is the best time. In a recent summer a family of five were seen almost daily only 50 yards above the houses in Alcombe Combe, near Minehead.

The fox is dog-shaped, but with a pointed muzzle, erect ears, and a handsome tail always known as the brush. An average height is 14 inches at the shoulder, and the length from tip of nose to end of brush just over 3 feet. The coat is a warm reddish-brown, white on the throat and underparts, and the reddish brush is tipped either black or white. In colour the sexes are alike, but the vixen is a few pounds lighter in weight. The eyes are bright and alert with intelligence and cunning, for the fox is well adapted for the hazards of hunting. Recently, one lay down in the middle of a ploughed field near Carhampton, with hounds and huntsmen searching the surrounding hedges and ditches. Five minutes after they had moved on, it sat up, looked around, and seeing the coast clear trotted off at a leisurely pace.

For food it depends largely on rats, mice, and rabbits. Hedgehogs, snails, frogs, and beetles are not despised, and neither is the occasional hen, pheasant, and more rarely a weakling lamb or newly-born deer calf. A certain amount of vegetable matter is also eaten, including grass and wild fruits, which on Exmoor usually means the whortleberry.

Otter

This animal of river and shore is rarely seen on Exmoor, though the Culmstock Otter Hounds make regular appearances in the National Park, chiefly in the Exe and Barle valleys. From time to time an angler or naturalist sitting quietly by any of the moorland streams may see an otter as it travels from pool to pool. It hunts mainly at nights, but in the lonelier parts of Exmoor it certainly moves about in the early evening long before the sun has set.

The male otter is called a dog, the female a bitch, and the cubs are born in a 'holt'. This is usually a convenient rabbit burrow, drain, or cavity under a tree root near to a river, and for the young it is lined with grass and reeds. They are born mainly in February and March, are blind for 35 days, and remain with their mother for almost a year. The dog otter leaves them shortly after birth, and continues his solitary ways. It is usually reckoned that each otter hunts a stretch of water about six miles long. He also frequents the shore, searching pools for fish, and turning over stones for crabs and other sea creatures.

An otter averages 4 feet in length, including the thick tail, and weighs about 23lbs. It has a double fur coat, an outer one of dusky brown, and a finer inner one, lighter in colour and water-proof. Surprisingly, it has a clear, soft, flute-like whistle, used for calling its mate or young at nights. It is a fine swimmer, and can dive superbly, but any food caught in the water is eaten on the bank-side or on a mid-stream rock. Fish, particularly eels and weaklings, is the main diet, and on land it takes mice, rabbits, insects, and snails. About 20 packs of Otter Hounds hunt in Britain, and some 200 otters are killed annually by various means. It survives because it is a great traveller, and has no permanent home, and so can move away from areas of severe persecution. In the National Park this is not too great, but the numbers are very small, and its continued existence is precarious.

Hare

This large cousin of the rabbit occurs over all the arable and grass lands of Exmoor, but is nowhere common. Apart from the mating season when the 'mad March Hare' dashes around at all hours, it rests in a 'form' until feeding time at dusk. The 'form' is usually made in a tuft of thick, dry grass among gorse or heather, but sometimes in an open field. Here the litter is born, normally from two to four, and the young leverets live in their own small 'forms' alongside the doe. Already at birth they have a coat of fur and open eyes, and after a month they are quite independent. The hare is a vegetarian, feeding on grass, clover, dandelions, sow-thistles, corn and root crops. The jack and doe are much alike in colour, dark brown with lighter streaks, a rufous tinge on the shoulders and sides, and whitish below. The young leveret is a more uniform brown. An adult is some 2 feet long, and weighs around 8lbs. It differs from the rabbit by its greater size, larger black-tipped ears, and the habit of living above ground and not in a burrow.

Rabbit

It is generally believed that rabbits came to Britain with the Romans. The Normans certainly protected them in special warrens or conygers as a valuable supply of fresh meat. The round Conygar Tower at Dunster stands upon an old warren, and the word 'coney' is derived from the Norman-French. Myxomatosis swept through Somerset in the mid-1950s as elsewhere in England, but the rabbit is back again in good numbers on Exmoor. Quite large colonies exist in many combes, and it is widespread over all farm land. In the more distant places its food consists only of grass and young shoots, but in the vale growing corn is also devoured and allotments are regularly visited. It is reckoned that five rabbits will eat as much vegetation as one sheep. 3lbs. is an average weight. An hour before dusk is a good time to see them as they come out to feed.

Red and Grey Squirrels

The Red Squirrel was fairly common in the oak and beech woods of Exmoor until the snowy winter of 1947. After this, numbers were drastically reduced, and it is doubtful if any are now left in the National Park. Some twenty years ago, the American Grey Squirrel started its invasion of West Somerset. This new squirrel spread rapidly into almost every wooded area, and now even the oak wood up Badgworthy Water has been colonized. It is always less common in coniferous woodlands, and prefers hardwood districts, parks, and orchards, where considerable damage is done through its eating the bark of young trees. The diet also includes fruit, nuts, beech-mast, and sometimes small birds, their eggs and nestlings. Early in the summer the young are born in a drey or nest of sticks, high up in the fork of a tall tree. Squirrels in England never fully hibernate in the winter.

Stoat and Weasel

The stoat is the larger of these two small hunting animals, and has a coat of reddish-brown with whitish underparts, and a black-tip to the long-haired tail. For food it kills rabbits, rats, mice, squirrels, and any ground nesting bird it can find. The weasel is of similar ferret-like shape, but the coat is redder, and the tail without the black tip. With an average length of 10 inches, it is four inches shorter than the stoat. It also feeds on rats, mice, voles, frogs and small birds. The stoat is more common on Exmoor than the weasel, but both are widespread.

Some Reptiles

SLOW-WORM

Classified with the lizards, but being without visible legs it resembles a snake. An adult can measure 18 inches long. The colour is silver-grey with a darker line down the centre of the back and along each side. It is very common in many grassy parts of Exmoor, and unfortunately large numbers are killed when the road verges are cut in June and July. The slow-worm is perfectly harmless, and feeds largely on slugs, earthworms and insects.

GRASS SNAKE

This is the largest of the British snakes. Adult females average 4 feet in length, and males about a foot less. It is quite harmless, carries no poison, and defends itself by hissing and ejecting a vile odour. On Exmoor it is usually found in damp places, but is scarce. It can best be distinguished from the smaller adder by the two yellow or orange patches just below the head. The general colouring is a uniform olive-grey, with a row of short black bars down each side.

ADDER

The adder is commonest on the dry moors and cliff-tops of Exmoor, but cases of snake-bite are very rare. It is not aggressive, and will always glide out of the way unless surprised basking in the sun. Due to the snake's small mouth, human fingers and toes are the most likely parts to be bitten. As a general precaution the ground should always be searched before sitting down in the open. 2 feet is the average length. The overall appearance varies from grey to brown, with a prominent black or dark brown zig-zag line down the back, and a line of dark spots on each side. Immediately behind the head is a dark V. Like all British snakes and lizards, it hibernates from October to March.

Birds

The variety of countryside within the National Park ensures a corresponding variety of birds, and at least 110 different species nest every year. In addition 26 species are regular winter visitors, and 24 occur as passage migrants. Also 84 have been recorded at some time or other as occasional or rare visitors, making a total of 244 species for the Exmoor Bird List.

BIRDS OF THE COAST AND HARBOURS

Most obvious and abundant are the Gulls; all Seagulls to many folk, and yet these Exmoor Gulls are made up of at least five different kinds. Here are some identification tips:

Herring Gull: large size, mantle of pearl grey, yellow bill with red spot on lower mandible. Very common and nests all along the coast.

Great Black-Backed Gull: easily the biggest Gull with a black mantle. Nests at Heddon's Mouth and Glenthorne.

57

Lesser Black-Backed Gull: plumage as above, but only the size of the Herring Gull. A few nest near Woody Bay, otherwise not often seen.

Black-Headed Gull: smallest of the regular Gulls, very common, but does not nest on Exmoor. The black hood is worn only in spring and summer, but at all seasons the adult has a white outer edge to wings, red legs and bill, and grey mantle.

Common Gull: regular winter visitor, especially to harbours and beaches. Like the Herring Gull, but legs and bill greenish and no red spot.

Mottled brown Gulls are all immature ones. Full plumage is not attained until the fourth or fifth year. The *Kittiwake* is a regular passage migrant, and other Gulls recorded include the *Little Gull, Glaucous Gull,* and *Sabine's Gull.* Another gull-like bird is the *Fulmar,* which nests in good numbers on the cliffs between Lynton and Combe Martin, together with about 1,000 pairs of *Razorbills* and *Guillemots.*

Resident Waders often seen along the shore are *Curlew, Redshank, Oystercatcher,* and *Ringed Plover.* Autumn and winter Waders include the *Turnstone, Dunlin, Sanderling, Little Stint, Greenshank, Golden Plover,* and the rarer *Black* and *Bar-tailed Godwits, Ruff, Spotted Redshank,* and *Whimbrel.* Three species of Duck breed on Exmoor, the lovely chestnut, black and white *Shelduck, Mallard,* and *Teal.* Winter visitors include the *Tufted Duck, Scaup, Pochard, Shoveler, Scoter, Pintail,* and the *Wigeon,* which is by far the most common of all.

BIRDS OF THE GARDENS, FIELDS, AND HEDGEROWS

Here is the highest density of birds with *Tits, Finches, Thrushes, Buntings, Warblers,* and *Pigeons* well represented. All the British members of the Tit family, except the rare *Bearded Tit,* occur on Exmoor, and though the *Willow Tit* is least known it certainly nests near Exford, and in Alcombe Combe, Minehead. Of the Finches, the *Chaffinch, Goldfinch, Bullfinch, Greenfinch,* and *Linnet* are common, the *Hawfinch* is very rare, while the *Brambling, Siskin, Twite,* and *Crossbill* are fairly regular winter visitors. The *Yellow Bunting* or *Yellowhammer* is well spread out along the hedges, and the scarce *Cirl Bunting* holds its own in the Bossington area.

Recently, many large gardens and sheltered spots have been colonized by the *Collared Dove,* while *Swallows, House Martins,* and *Swifts* are summer visitors to all Exmoor villages. The *Spotted Flycatcher* inhabits many a farmyard. A few pairs of *Barn Owls* and *Little Owls* manage to breed each year, but their numbers have been small for some years past. Rookeries are widespread, and usually not too far from human habitation. Parks with tall trees are sure to have the mouse-like *Treecreeper,* and the lovely

Nuthatch. Robin, Wren, Hedge Sparrow, Blackbird, Song Thrush, Starling, House Sparrow are all garden birds, and the Scandinavian nesting *Fieldfare* and *Redwing* are common in the fields over the winter.

BIRDS OF THE WOODS AND STREAMS

The three British resident *Woodpeckers* nest in Exmoor woodlands, the *Green* with its laughing call, and the drumming *Great* and *Lesser Spotted*. The *Green* is not so wedded to the woods as its two cousins, and is often seen on the moors and cliffs in search of ants. The *Heron* vies with the fisherman on all the rivers and streams, and there is a heronry of about twenty nests in the woods at Coppleham Cross, near Winsford. The *Dipper* haunts all the streams with the *Grey Wagtail* (the underparts are yellow) and a few pairs of *Kingfishers*.

Trees with holes are favourite nesting places, and in the oak woods these are used by *Jackdaws, Stock Doves*, and *Tawny Owls*. Smaller holes attract the *Redstart, Pied Flycatcher*, the various *Tits, Treecreeper* and *Nuthatch*. Often seen and heard on the outskirts of woods are the *Chiff-chaff, Wood* and *Willow Warblers*, and in the newer growth there are usually *Blackcaps, Whitethroats*, and a few Garden *Warblers*. The *Nightjar* seems especially drawn to woodlands adjacent to moors, and often nests under a pile of dead branches in a clearing. *Buzzards* and *Ravens* are some of Exmoor's largest and most interesting birds, and though a few nest along the cliffs, they usually select the top of a sturdy tree. The *Kestrel* is quite common, and often takes over an old *Crow's* nest for breeding, but the scarcer *Sparrow Hawk* prefers to build in conifers.

BIRDS OF THE HIGHER COMBES AND MOORS

Almost any one of the higher combes with a stream and a few trees is a popular summer place for birds. Here will be *Whinchats*, probably a pair of *Stonechats, Willow Warblers*, and the resident *Wren, Dipper* and *Grey Wagtail*. Many of these combes have a pair or two of *Ring Ouzels*, almost certainly *Wheatears* if there is a stone wall or some rocks nearby. A select few will have a pair of nesting *Merlins*, the smallest and most dashing of all British Falcons. Most of Exmoor's *Crows* frequent these upland valleys, and their stick and wool-lined nest will be found in many a thorn bush. The *Mistle Thrush, Robin, Chaffinch, Great Tit, Tree Pipit*, and sometimes the *Kestrel*, are all well represented among the nesting population, but the great majoirty only stay for the summer months.

On open moorland, the *Meadow Pipit* is the most abundant bird at all times of the year, and it is much put upon by the *Cuckoo* at nesting time. The *Cuckoo* is quite common during May and June over much of the National Park, but seems to prefer the moors, particularly if there is a good beech hedge at hand. *Curlews*, and some *Lapwings*, come up from the beaches to nest on the moors, and join the *Skylarks* and *Ring Ouzels* in the dawn and evening chorus. On heather slopes the *Red Grouse* nests in small numbers, and a few *Black Grouse* are still about. In some of the boggy places the *Snipe* is regularly seen, often with the *Reed Bunting* not too far away. Autumn brings the *Short-eared Owl* and *Woodcock* to favoured spots, *Harriers* are reported from time to time, and there are a few *Snow Buntings* and *Black Redstarts* every winter.

See N. V. Allen's Microstudy, *The Birds of Exmoor*. For a short section on Birdwatching see Chapter 6 of this book.

Wild Plants

Something like 800 varieties of wild plants come into flower every year within the National Park. They are at their best throughout June and July when hundreds of different kinds bedeck the countryside. Reference has already been made in Chapter 2 to the main constituents of moorland vegetation—grass and heather in particular—so the following section will be devoted to a brief glance at some of the wild flowers, familiar though many of them are in most parts of the English countryside.

Before March is out *Primroses* appear along the sheltered banks, but it is well into April before the glorious masses appear. About the same time *Common Gorse*, which flowers for much of the year, shines like patches of bright sun on the brown hillsides. May is the month when *Cow Parsley* curtains the roadsides, standing tall above the *Stitchworts*, *Herb Robert*, *Speedwell*, and *Red Campion*. *Hawthorn* and *Blackthorn* blossom in the hedgerows by late May, but in the upland combes it is several weeks later before they flower, and usually at the same time as the *Rowan* or *Mountain Ash*.

Foxgloves flourish well on Exmoor, and they often stand like sentinels in full-dress, thousands in a row, lining many woodland paths and moorland streams. *Honeysuckle* is familiar, not only in the hedgerows, but by the streams running down from the hills. Near the water's edge, *Meadow Sweet*, *Forget-me-not*, *Water Mint*, and *Lady's Smock* are all quite common among the rushes and tall grasses.

In damp and boggy places the *Heath Spotted Orchid* is constantly found, and there are places where hundreds grow together. The *Marsh Orchid* occurs on the lower grasslands, and the *Early Purple* is scattered in thin woodland. Rarer Orchids which have been recorded are the *Butterfly*, *Bird's Nest*, *Fragrant*, and *Pyramidal*. Whenever any of these Orchids, or any of the rarer flowers are found, they should on no account be picked, or worse still, dug out by the roots or bulb.

Cotton Grass, with its nodding white tufts, the attractive yellow *Bog Asphodel*, the *Bog Violet* and *Bog Pimpernel*, all grow on moorland wet spots, and among the *Bog Moss* or *Sphagnum* of The Chains the scarce insect-eating *Round-leaved Sundew* flourishes. Porlock Marsh, with its huge shingle ridge to hold back the sea, is an interesting place for plants. These include not only several Orchids, and the usual coastal *Thrift, Samphire, Sea Spurry*, and *Aster*, but also the *Arrowhead, Yellow Flag, Horned Poppy*, and the *Musky Stork's Bill*.

Great masses of pink *Rosebay Willow-herb* grow by the roadside, especially in southern Exmoor. Towards the end of July it stands higher than the hedges in some places along the Exford—Simonsbath road. August is the month of the 'purple headed mountain' with acres of heather aglow on Dunkery, Winsford Hill, Brendon Common, and countless other hilltops. In many places the *Whortleberry* or *Bilberry* grows well among the heather, and September is the time for picking 'Urts' and Blackberries.

Trees

Although Exmoor has never been particularly known for forestry, yet for a moorland region it is remarkably well wooded. The prevalence of oak, as coppice or scrub, encouraged charcoal burning and tan barking in the past, while there has always been sufficient timber—even if inferior in quality—for fencing and day-to-day farm use. Trees, too, have served a useful purpose as boundary marks, e.g. the Hoar Oak in the old Royal Forest, last re-planted in 1916 and still standing today. Several churchyards and cross-roads boast specimens of great age, size and girth, a notable example being the sycamore at Dulverton, known as the Belfry Tree.

Private parks at Pixton (Dulverton), Dunster, and Nettlecombe, with hardwoods up to 200 years old, still flourish, while Birch Cleave planted by the Knight family in the 1840s contains some of the highest *beech* trees in the country—most of them now past their prime. The most remarkable of all the amenity woods are those founded by Sir Thomas Acland at Holnicote in the early 19th century. Between 1810 and 1826 he planted about 800,000 trees, many of them evergreen oaks, in separate sections to commemorate the births of his children. Forming part of the National Trust holding on Exmoor today, they stand in a vast concourse accessible to all, a form of landscape architecture and husbandry of the most impressive kind.

Other landowners on Exmoor showed forestry enterprise in the 19th century. At Glenthorne on the coast, the Rev. W. Stevenson Halliday planted Monterey cypress for shelter belts, and clothed the combes with beech, larch, and Scots and Corsican pines. Later he planted Yenworthy and Stag's Head woods, and established an experimental pinetum. At Dunster, Mr. Alexander Fownes Luttrell pioneered Sitka spruce and Douglas fir—some of the latter species, planted in 1874, are now over 150 feet in height, with girths of 12 feet or more.

Since the end of the First World War, the Forestry Commission has become the chief forestry authority and operator in Britain. Its main holding in Exmoor is the Brendon Forest, 3,000 acres in extent, covering Croydon and Kennisham Hills, south-east of Dunster. Here, as at Holnicote, the public is being encouraged to respect and enjoy the amenities provided by the trees—a form of multiple use made increasingly available as the plantations mature.

See Roger Miles' Microstudy, *The Trees and Woods of Exmoor*.

Valley of the Rocks, Lynton.

6 Recreation and Amenities

The Exmoor National Park Authorities have prepared a number of leaflets about Exmoor. These include lists of Riding Stables, Youth Hostels, Motoring, Touring Caravan and Tent sites, as well as information about the archaeology, churches, geology, and wild life of the National Park. Also available are some excellent publications on rights-of-way and kindred subjects noted below.

Devon and Somerset County Councils have each appointed a Warden to look after National Park business in the field. The advice of these two knowledgeable and helpful officers is always available.

Walking

Strongly recommended are two booklets with maps and text published by the Somerset County Council. These are *Waymarked Walks* 1 and *Waymarked Walks* 2, price 20p. each. Devon County Council has produced a parallel range of leaflets covering the Lynton to Combe Martin section of the Park. The prime value of these guides lies in the fact that you can follow approved routes without fear of trespass.

Several Exmoor Rambling and Walking Clubs organise regular excursions across the moors. Although there are wet places on Exmoor, especially on hill slopes, and around the headwaters of rivers and streams, there are no dangerous bogs, in spite of the rumour that Farmer Mole and his horse were swallowed up at Mole's Chamber! For any long walk over open moorland it is important to wear stout, waterproof boots, and to carry a good map and compass. The special Exmoor Tourist One-inch Ordnance Survey map is highly recommended. Two long distance paths should be noted. One is the S.W. Peninsular Coast Path which starts at Minehead and—with breaks—follows the coastline to Combe Martin and beyond. The other—designed to link Dartmoor and Exmoor—is in preparation.

Horse Riding and Pony Trekking

Exmoor is superb riding country with miles of bridle paths and moorland tracks well away from motor traffic. A number of farmhouses and hotels cater especially for riding holidays, while most towns and villages on or near Exmoor have riding stables. Most of these stables give basic and elementary instruction, and there are a few that include advanced teaching, dressage, and jumping. British Olympic riders have trained more than once at a school in the Porlock Vale. Riders are usually accompanied by an experienced horseman from the stables, or escorts can be arranged on request.

For details apply to the Information Centres, or study the advertisements in *The Exmoor Review*.

Hunting

The weekly *West Somerset Free Press* publishes a full list of all Hunting Appointments or Meets of the various packs. The paper also reports the hunting in some detail. Visitors anxious to hunt should contact a local riding stable where all the necessary information, and often a suitable horse, can be secured.

The earliest record of staghounds on Exmoor relates to a pack kept by Sir Hugh Pollard, Warden of the Forest, near the end of the 16th century. But regular hunting with horses and hounds did not start until about 1750, and by the end of the century it was particularly vigorous under the mastership of Sir Thomas Acland and Colonel Basset. Difficult days around 1820 led to the sale of the strongly built staghounds, the only pack of its kind in the country. After a short lapse, during which the deer suffered much from poachers, the present Devon and Somerset Staghounds was established with kennels at Exford. Today, the enthusiasm and support has never been stronger, and the chase of the wild red deer has made Exford the hunting capital of the moor.

Stags of 5 years and older are hunted from August to October, and young stags of about 3 years in the spring. The harbourer, a local man with specialised knowledge of deer, locates the quarry and informs the Master. Then about four pairs of mature hounds, the tufters, are taken out to rouse the stag, and separate it from the others. With this achieved, the rest of the pack are set on the line of scent, and the contest begins. The stag is not always brought to bay, but when this happens it is not attacked by the hounds, but quickly dispatched by shooting. Throughout the winter hinds are hunted, and then the harbourer is not used. Point-to-Point races are held in April and May in connection with the various hunts.

The relevant addresses are:—

Devon and Somerset Staghounds. Kennels at Exford.
Exmoor Foxhounds. Kennels at Simonsbath.
Dulverton East. Kennels at East Anstey.
Dulverton West. Kennels at North Molton.
West Somerset Foxhounds. Kennels at Carhampton.
Minehead Harriers. Kennels at Wootton Courtenay.

Bird Watching

In many ways this is the complete recreation, for it can be followed throughout life, at all seasons of the year, and in almost every place. On Exmoor especially, it means healthy exercise in the pure air sweeping in from the Atlantic, the delights of the sheltered combes or open moors, and there is always the chance of seeing red deer, foxes, and the rare otter, as well as the many birds.

Only a few items of equipment are necessary for Bird Watching; good binoculars, a magnification of 8 x 40 are best; a book illustrating British birds in colour—there are several suitable ones costing around £1.50—or the writer's *Birds of Exmoor* in black and white in the Microstudy series, listing all the 244 birds seen in the National Park; a small notebook for the pocket, and another larger one for writing up permanent records. Warm clothing, a good pair of boots, and maps, complete the Bird Watcher's outfit.

Exmoor has dozens, indeed hundreds, of good bird haunts, found in four main areas; the coastal beaches, cliffs, and headlands; the gardens, fields, lanes and hedgerows; the woodlands and streams; the higher combes and moors. April to July is the best time for watching nesting birds, but the spring and autumn migration, especially along the coast, is also full of interest. Rare birds are reported occasionally, and in recent years these have included the *Kite, Nutcracker, Lapland Bunting, Great Grey Shrike*, and various ducks and waders along the coast. The National Park has a wide variety of birds, and some twenty of the regular nesting birds are either very scarce or unknown in many other parts of England. For the beginner, and for the experienced Bird Watcher, Exmoor has a great deal to offer and to delight.

River and Sea Fishing

Of the various branches of angling, Exmoor offers fine opportunities for game and sea fishing, but there is practically no coarse fishing. River Board licences for Somerset and Devon, covering both trout and salmon, are available at the Minehead Publicity Office, and most fishing tackle shops. Stretches of game fishing are, of course, either privately or publicly owned, and advice on obtaining tickets can be had from any of the Information Centres, tackle shops, and most country hotels.

Small Brown Trout abound in all the rivers and streams, but they are a hungry and wary lot. A 10-inch fish weighing 4 ozs. is a good average, though occasionally the half-pounder is landed. Nicholas Snow, of Oare, once tried to beat Parson Froude's record of 315 trout caught in a single day. Setting out on a June morning at 5.30 a.m. he filled several baskets with fish, but his total catch at the end of the day was only 265! The season runs from 15 March to 30 September, but the middle three months are generally the best.

A few Rainbow Trout and Grayling are sometimes caught in the southern streams, and Nutscale reservoir, above Porlock, has been stocked with both Rainbow and Brown Trout.

The Salmon season extends from 14 February to 30 September, but it is usually the end of April before any appear in the Exmoor rivers. Good numbers run up the East Lyn, and most of the large streams, as well as the Barle and Exe, have their quota. A few Sea Trout also appear from time to time. There has been some decline in recent years of Exmoor Salmon, due partly to disease, and partly to more intensive sea-fishing by Continental countries.

Rubber boots will usually keep the fisherman dry shod at marshy spots and tributary streams, but wading in thigh boots is always essential in the clear rivers of the moor. Many of the moorland waters run through deep valleys, the hillsides covered in bracken, heather, or rough grass. Horned sheep, the dipper, wren, and grey wagtail will be the fisherman's companions, and the grey heron his rival.

See H. B. Maund's Microstudy, *The Fish of Exmoor*.

Excellent sea fishing can be had along much of the Exmoor coast, with cod, bass, whiting, conger, skate, and mackerel, all well reported. Some of the stony beaches and rocky headlands can be hard on tackle, and many good places are limited by the state of the tide. Care should always be taken to avoid getting cut-off by the incoming tide on low water sand patches and rocky ledges. Most of the harbour entrances, sea walls, and open beaches offer good fishing, and for those anxious to go after heavier fish, boats can be hired at Minehead, Porlock Weir, Lynmouth, and Combe Martin.

Sailing

Exmoor's rugged coast, the fast running currents in the Bristol Channel, and the frequent strong west winds bringing in the Atlantic rollers, limit the amount of sailing possible. Even so, there are often excellent conditions for dinghies, and the standard competitive boat in use is the 14-foot long, clinker built, *Yachting World* 'Dayboat'. Throughout the season, dinghy races are arranged for most weekends, plus a few for sailing cruisers. There are anchorages in the harbours at Minehead, Porlock Weir, Lynmouth, Combe Martin, and Watermouth Bay, but these all dry out at low water, so it is essential to check the state of the tide when planning to enter. Arrowsmith's *Bristol Channel Tide Tables*, published yearly, is a handy little book for all sailing enthusiasts. Additional information can always be obtained from the various Harbour Masters.

Minehead has a flourishing sailing club with premises near the harbour, and a membership of over 100. Beginners are always welcomed, and so are members of clubs affiliated to the R.Y.A. Just beyond the National Park at Watermouth Castle, between

Combe Martin and Ilfracombe, there is an expanding marina with hotel accommodation, and facilities for caravans and camping, in addition to sailing.

Lifeboats are stationed at Minehead and Ilfracombe, and the only Exmoor lighthouse is on Foreland Point, Countisbury, first lit in 1900. This is open to the public each weekday from 1.0 p.m. to one hour before sunset. The light is a White Light Group Flashing (4) every 15 seconds, and the Fog Signal, Blast 2 seconds, Silent 2 seconds; Blast 2 seconds, Silent 2 seconds; Blast 2 seconds, Silent 20 seconds.

Youth Hostels and Camping

The Youth Hostels Association (Y.H.A.) has three Hostels within Exmoor National Park: at Alcombe, Minehead; Exe Mead, Exford; and Lynbridge, Lynton. There are also two beyond the eastern boundary at Crowcombe and Holford, and another has recently closed at the Old Malthouse, Bampton. These are just five of over 250 Hostels in England and Wales controlled by the Y.H.A. with the object of encouraging young people to explore the countryside. Good hostel type accommodation is provided at reasonable prices, with some meals and cooking facilities. They are usually closed during the day until 5 p.m. and a stay is normally limited to three successive nights. It is always advisable to book in advance whenever possible.

A list is also available showing some twenty sites on Exmoor where camping is permitted. In addition, farmers and owners may allow camping on their land, subject to their own inclination and a limited stay. A fine site on North Hill, Minehead, is run by the Camping Club. Bye-laws of the National Trust forbid camping on any of their land outside of the regular sites. It is important to remark that the whole of Exmoor is owned by someone, and that an open stretch of moorland is as private in this respect as a fenced field.

Motoring

Driving in the National Park calls for special care owing to the steep hills, and the narrow and unfenced roads. Hills such as Porlock and Countisbury have a gradient in places of 1 in 4, and many of the more isolated country roads are just as steep. None is really difficult or dangerous provided the roadside signs to engage bottom gear are obeyed. On narrow and twisting roads always travel slowly, keep well to the left-hand side, and be prepared to stop at a moment's notice. Look out for the passing places, and be willing to pull-in or reverse into one.

Sheep are a great hazard on unfenced roads, especially on the A.39 Porlock to Lynton road. Here they often feed or shelter along

the verges, and frequently cross over from one side to the other.
Many are injured or killed every year, usually because the motorist
has been going too fast.

Having sounded this note of warning, it can also be said with
confidence that here is some of the best motoring in Britain.
Parking places are frequent along most roads, especially above
Porlock Hill to Lynmouth where there are fine land and seascapes;
likewise between Lynmouth and Simonsbath where the road runs
through the heart of the moors. Parking space is also provided
at most of the beauty spots, e.g. Dunster, Selworthy, Porlock Weir,
Oare Water, Tarr Steps, Winsford Hill, Landacre Bridge, Trentishoe Down, Hunter's Inn, and by the river Barle near Pinkworthy
Farm. Adequate parking is also provided in all the small towns,
and near the seafront at Minehead.

Much of Exmoor can be seen from a car even if all its delights
and pursuits cannot be experienced. Details of suggested motor
tours and car trails are available at the Exmoor Information Centres.

Caravans

Many of the Exmoor roads are quite unsuitable for towed caravans
as reversing is a frequent necessity. The A.396 Tiverton to Minehead is adequate apart from a couple of tricky corners in Dunster,
and so is the A.39 Bridgwater to Minehead. Beyond Minehead the
A.39 has the very steep hills at Porlock and Countisbury, but the
former can be avoided by taking the Toll Road. At Blackmoor
Gate the A.399 runs down to Combe Martin and on to Ilfracombe—a section without special difficulties. These are the only
A class roads within the National Park. Of the B roads, the B.3223
Dulverton to Simonsbath and Lynmouth; B.3224 Wheddon Cross
to Exford; B.3358 Simonsbath to Challacombe and Blackmoor
Gate, are all without major problems. There are some fourteen
touring caravan sites in or near the National Park, and a list is
obtainable from the Exmoor Information Centres.

Lousewort

7 Gazetteer

Over 100 places are listed in this section, and include all the villages and many historic buildings, monuments and points of interest. An Ordnance Survey Map Reference is supplied with each entry.

ALDERMAN'S BARROW 837423. Bronze Age round barrow by roadside N. of Exford. Once a boundary mark of the Royal Forest. A good starting point for walks to Larkbarrow and Badgworthy Water, Chalk and Weir Water.

ALLERFORD 905470. Domesday hamlet in the parish of Selworthy, with a much photographed packhorse bridge. Small car park and toilets. The narrow road continues on to Bossington, and then by a rough track to the sea.

ARLINGTON COURT 605405. National Trust property in N. Devon. Open to public daily April to mid-October. Furnished Regency house with Miss Chichester's collection of model ships, shells, and old pewter. Horse drawn vehicles in stable block.

BADGWORTHY WATER 792477. A lovely and most famous valley in the Doone country. Best approach is from Malmsmead, where there is a large car park, toilets, and refreshments. Two miles up Badgworthy is Hoccombe Combe, the Doone valley.

BARBROOK 715477. Hamlet delightfully situated on West Lyn river, two miles S. of Lynton on A.39. Overshadowed by Beggar's Roost, 1,000 feet high.

BARLYNCH ABBEY 929290. Medieval monastic remains between A.396 road and river Exe, one mile N. of Dulverton.

BEULAH CHAPEL 027344. Old Methodist mining chapel at an isolated road junction on Brendon Hills one mile W. of Raleigh's Cross. Weekly service still held.

BOSSINGTON 898478. An ancient hamlet which in Saxon days belonged to the abbey of Athelney. Lies between Allerford and the sea, mainly owned by National Trust. Its early 16th century Lynch Chapel was restored in 1885 after being used as a barn.

BRATTON 947463. Sheltered wooded hamlet one mile W. of Minehead. Bratton Court is a medieval manor house.

BRENDON 760477. Pop. 213. Not to be looked for in the Brendon Hills, but by the East Lyn river just inside the Devon border. Delightful valley setting, a great haunt of anglers and walkers. Called after St. Brendan the Voyager, a much travelled Irish saint. Apart from its Norman font, the church (rebuilt in 1873) is remarkable for its distance from the village—nearly two miles and 700 feet up.

BRENDON TWO GATES 765433. Modern cattle grid on Simonsbath—Lynton B.3223 road now bridges the gap in the old Forest wall, once closed by a double gate. Suitable off-road parking. Good place for walking E. down Hoccombe Water, or W. to Hoar Oak Tree. Memorial stone on Brendon Common in N.E. direction to Col. R. H. Maclaren killed on duty here in 1941.

BRIDGETOWN 924333. Hamlet by river Exe in parish of Exton on A.396 midway between Wheddon Cross and Dulverton. Has a delightful riverside cricket pitch.

BROCKWELL 929430. Cluster of farm buildings and a few houses at foot of Robin Howe in parish of Wootton Courtenay. A peaceful spot where the Badger, or Brock, still flourishes.

BROMPTON REGIS 954314. Pop. 442. Quietly set in hill country well away from modern traffic, between the Brendons and Haddon Hill. Once held personally by William the Conqueror. 'Brompton' indicates a settlement surrounded by broom, a yellow flowering shrub.

BRUSHFORD 920258. Pop. 496. In sheltered valley, close to river Barle, three miles S. of Dulverton. The church, with its monuments and chapel built by Lutyens in 1926, is well worth a visit.

BURGUNDY CHAPEL 947482. Ruined chapel or hermitage built about 1500 probably to fulfil a vow made at a time of great peril. Reached in an hour by track leading W. from Minehead quay along seaward side of North Hill.

BURY 945275. Pretty hamlet in lower Haddeo valley near Dulverton. Deep ford and V.R. letter box. Bury Castle is Norman.

CARATACUS STONE 890335. Inscribed stone of the Dark Ages. Under a stone shelter near Spire Cross on Winsford Hill. Plenty of parking on this National Trust land.

CARHAMPTON 100425. Pop. 779. Last village on A.39 before Minehead is reached. Once sufficiently important to give its name to the Hundred or Administrative Centre of 18 parishes. Now a quiet village, with traces of its olden links. Custom of apple-wassailing observed annually on 17th January.

CHAINS, THE 735418. Map reference is for Chains Barrow, 1,599 feet, the highest point. Exmoor's central wilderness of water-logged deer sedge; headwaters of the Exe, Barle, and Lyn rivers. Approached either from Pinkworthy Pond, the easiest, or from Brendon Two Gates via Hoar Oak Tree, and Long Chains Combe.

CHALLACOMBE 694410. Pop. 153. A moorland village, the name means 'cold valley', two miles inside Devon on the B.3358. The inn has the intriguing name of 'The Black Venus'.

CHAPMAN BARROWS 695434. Group of 11 Bronze Age burial mounds above Challacombe. Extensive all-round views.

CLEEVE ABBEY 047407. Remains of Cistercian Abbey, open to public. Near village of Washford.

CLOUTSHAM 892431. Farm, stream, and woodlands below Dunkery. Parking above and below farm buildings. Good centre for picnics and walks. Richard of Cloutsham was surety for a man when the King's justices were at Ilchester in 1242.

COMBE MARTIN 585465. Pop. 2420. Early Closing Wednesday. Village started around the old silver mines a mile inland and gradually crept down the valley to the sea. Named from Martin de Turon, friend of William the Conqueror. Interesting 15th century church, and quaint 'Pack of Cards' inn. Market gardening and tourism main occupations. Exmoor Information Centre open in Harbour Car Park from Easter to October.

COMBEROW 028353. A remote corner of the Brendons, and once a station on the old Brendon Hills Mineral Line. Reached by a narrow, winding road off the B.3190 or by footpath from Roadwater.

COUNTISBURY 747488. Pop. 80. This hamlet has probably never had more than its present dozen ancient cottages, 16th century 'Blue Ball' inn, and church. Exmoor's largest Iron Age fort on hill to the W. Here Odda of Devon defeated the Danes in 878 A.D.

COUNTY GATE 794487. Somerset—Devon boundary on A.39. Large car park and toilets. Fine views into moors, and over Glenthorne to sea.

COW CASTLE 795373. Isolated Iron Age fort overlooking Barle. Can be reached either by walking up from Landacre Bridge or down from Simonsbath.

COWLEY WOOD 644445. Newly formed Conservation Centre with nature trail. Admission by appointment. Phone Parracombe 200.

CROYDON HILL 975405. Wooded part of Brendon Hills, traversed by Dunster—Luxborough road. Highest point 1,197 feet. Parking and picnic area, and fine walks.

CULBONE 843483. Pop. 27. No public road goes to Culbone, and it is best approached by a woodland path from above Porlock Weir. Tiny Gothic church, set in a deep valley, is the smallest complete church in England.

CUTCOMBE 932394. Pop. 330. The main activity of the parish is centred at Wheddon Cross with the combined shop and post office, cattle market, and 'Rest and Be Thankful' inn. The recently restored church stands on the edge of the Brendons, half-a-mile to the E.

DOONE VALLEY 793444. See Badgworthy Water.

DULVERTON 915280. Pop. 1,392. Early Closing Thursday. Quiet little town of narrow streets by the Barle. Rural District offices in old workhouse. The Saxon name means 'settlement by the ford over the bend'. First class centre for fishing, riding, walking, and exploring southern Exmoor. Sir George Williams, founder of the Y.M.C.A., was born at nearby Ashway Farm in 1821. Offices of Exmoor Society in Parish Rooms, open Tuesday and Saturday, 10.30—12.30 p.m.

DUNKERY BEACON 891416. 1,705 feet, highest point of Exmoor and Somerset. Fire beacon station in olden days. Now National Trust. Easy walk of mile from moorland road to the summit. Tremendous views on clear days.

DUNSTER 990437. Pop. 958. This famous tripartite village of castle, church, and dwellings, is near-perfect as the modern car will permit. With old Yarn Market, Luttrell Arms, once the residence of the Abbot of Cleeve 500 years ago, and 15th century church full of interest. Car park on Minehead side, and small one near Gallox Packhorse bridge.

ELWORTHY 083350. Pop. 82. Quiet village on B.3188 Watchet—Wiveliscombe road. Its name means the 'old village', and the manor was given to William de Mohun, of Dunster, by the Conqueror.

EXE HEAD 752413. Source of river Exe in boggy ground 1,500 feet up on E. edge of The Chains.

EXFORD 855384. Pop. 450. On river Exe in the heart of the National Park. Busy hunting, fishing and walking centre, with several large hotels and Youth Hostel. The hill-top church has a fine screen brought from St. Audries, and the Methodist chapel two brilliant Burne-Jones windows. Annual Horse Show second Wednesday in August.

EXTON 926337. Pop. 248. An old Domesday settlement. The present church and few houses are built up on a steep slope east of the A.396. Post office and shop are down at Bridgetown by the Exe.

FARLEY WATER 741478. Map ref. is for its junction with Hoaroak Water at Hillsford Bridge. A long moorland combe running almost due N. from Exe Plain, 1,450 feet up. Park off B.3223 at Shilstone Hill, walk due W. and drop into Farley combe, a lovely stretch of great beauty.

FIVE BARROWS 733368. Actually there are eight, of the Bronze Age period and 1,618 feet high. To right of Simonsbath—Brayford road at Kinsford Gate.

FORELAND POINT 755510. Purchased by National Trust in December 1971. Precipitous cliffs and footpath to Exmoor's only lighthouse.

FORTESCUE MEMORIAL 759380. Stone cairn by roadside W. of Simonsbath—Kinsford Gate road, to author of 'History of British Army' and 'The Story of a Red Deer'.

GLENTHORNE 798497. Fine section of wooded coast, privately owned, below County Gate. Nature Trail goes down to beach.

GRABBIST 980435. Four-mile range of hills rising to 970 feet between Dunster and Wootton Courtenay. Extensive views to Dunkery, Brendons, and over Minehead to Bristol Channel.

GREAT HANGMAN 600480. Massive down, 1,044 feet high, overlooking Combe Martin and the sea.

HAWKRIDGE 862306. Pop. 51. A lonely village set nearly 1,000 feet above Danes Brook and the Barle. Best reached from Dulverton. The church has a Norman doorway, and white-washed interior. The buzzard, with its four-feet wing-span, is the chief hawk here today.

HEASLEY MILL 735323. Hamlet with a fine old guest house in Mole valley and near the disused Bampfylde mine. This and other mines worked extensively in last century. Some derelict buildings and slag heaps remain.

HEDDON'S MOUTH 655497. Wild section of coast between Martinhoe and Trentishoe reached by mile-long path from Hunter's Inn.

HOAR OAK TREE 748430. Ancient boundary mark of Exmoor Forest near wall by Hoaroak Water. Present tree planted in 1916. Follow wall W. from Brendon Two Gates over two miles of hilly country.

HORNER 899454. Cluster of houses in Luccombe parish by Horner Water at foot of Dunkery. Name is said to derive from Saxon 'hwrnwr'—the snorer, on account of its gurgling stream. Picturesque woodland walk by the water to Cloutsham or Webber's Post. Large car park.

HURLSTONE POINT 898494. E. Point of Porlock Bay with coastguard lookout. This rocky headland is a good workshop for marine biology, but beware of incoming tide.

ILFRACOMBE 520475. Pop. 8,210. Early closing Thursday. Largest resort on this rocky N. Devon coast, six miles beyond National Park. The Victorian town looks out over mouth of Bristol Channel between Hillsborough, Lantern, and Capstone hills. Has a number of small sandy beaches, sheltered gardens, harbour, and small museum.

LANDACRE BRIDGE 816362. 16th century bridge over Barle at foot of Withypool Common. Car park. Quiet riverside strolls or more strenuous walk up to Iron Age Cow Castle.

LARKBARROW 820429. A ruined Knight farm on the moorland track from Alderman's Barrow to Badgworthy Water.

LEIGHLAND CHAPEL 033365. Isolated hamlet with church restored in 1862, and once belonging to Cleeve Abbey. Situated in Brendon foothills midway between Roadwater and Raleigh's Cross.

LONGSTONE 705431. Finest of Exmoor's Bronze Age standing stones, 9½ feet tall. On a desolate stretch of the moor between Wood Barrow on the old Forest boundary and Chapman Barrows.

LUCCOMBE 910445. Pop. 189. The prefix 'luc' has the same meaning as 'lock' in Porlock. One is the 'enclosed valley' the other the 'enclosed port'. Most of the village belongs to the National Trust, and hamlets of Horner and West Luccombe are included in the parish. A survey was published in 1947 under the title *Exmoor Village*, by W. J. Turner. Beautifully set among trees at the bottom of Robin Howe.

LUCKWELL BRIDGE 905387. Hamlet on Wheddon Cross—Exford road in parish of Cutcombe. The bridge is over the Quarme, which in 1830 turned two mills here. Early Bible Christian chapel still used for weekly services.

LUXBOROUGH 974380. Pop. 182. Set among the Brendon Hills where it is said the Romans once mined iron ore. Reached either from Dunster or by a turning near Raleigh's Cross. Church has an unusual saddle-back slate roof tower. Post office is in the hamlet of Kingsbridge, a mile away.

LYNMOUTH 725495. Pop. with Lynton 1,981. Built alongside river and sea it is justly famous for its fine situation. Lovely walks through woodlands to Watersmeet. Connected with Lynton by a cliff railway 300 yards long.

LYNTON 720495. Early closing Thursday. This has Domesday links, but the little town is quaintly Victorian, built on an uneven platform amid encircling hills. A popular holiday centre with a spectacular cliff walk of a mile to Valley of Rocks. Information centre in Lee Road, and museum in St. Vincent's cottage.

MALMSMEAD 791477. Hamlet at junction of Oare and Badgworthy forming East Lyn river. Easiest starting point for walk to Doone Valley. Large car park.

MARTINHOE 668487. Pop. 149. Small village set among the hills near N. Devon coast. Bishop Hannington, killed in E. Africa in 1885, was curate here.

MINEHEAD 970465. Pop. 8,063. Early Closing Wednesday. Chief holiday resort in W. Somerset. Arms of the town are a ship under sail and a wool pack, indicative of its former trade. Wide shopping centre in the Parade and Avenue. Important church dedicated to St. Michael. Hobby horse parades the district on May Day with dancing attendants.

MOLLAND 808284. Pop. 242. Lies just outside S. boundary of National Park looking down into Yeo valley. 15th century church with 18th century interior of outstanding interest.

MONKSILVER 073374. Pop. 101. Rural village in pretty valley on B.3188. 'Silver' comes from Latin 'silva' indicating a wooded district. A mile away is Combe Sydenham, from where the daughter Elizabeth married Sir Francis Drake.

NEGUS STONE 696437. Memorial stone to Robin Negus, who died in 1932 aged 17½. Near the most westerly Chapman barrow.

NETTLECOMBE 056378. Pop. 201. The old church is full of interest, and the Court, a 16th century building, was long the home of the Trevelyans. It is now a Field Study centre.

NORTH HILL, MINEHEAD 940478. Immediately W. of town overlooking Bristol Channel with fine scenic road to Selworthy Beacon, 1,013 feet.

NUTSCALE RESERVOIR 860433. Bottom of Chetsford Water, covers 24 acres and supplies Minehead.

OARE 802473. Pop. 57. Famous for its church where Lorna Doone was married to Jan Ridd in Blackmore's novel, and for the beauty of its setting. The name signifies a 'limit' or 'boundary' for the parish abuts on to Devonshire. Hoar Oak, a well-known Forest boundary mark, also has the same meaning. Parish has neither shop, post office, nor telephone booth.

PARRACOMBE 670450. Pop. 309. Built on a steep slope below Lynton—Barnstaple road. River Heddon, little more than a brook here, flows across the bottom. Norman church of St. Petrock recently preserved. From the late Victorian church near centre of village there is a good view of Holwell Castle, a small Norman earth fort.

PINKWORTHY POND 724424. Constructed by John Knight about 1840 on edge of The Chains. Walk up from B.3358 passing Pinkworthy Farm.

PORLOCK 885468. Pop. 1,307. Early closing Wednesday. Encircled by hills except on seaward side, the parish includes Porlock Weir and Porlock West. A large busy village with roots deep in the past. Church of St. Dubricius contains fine monuments.

PORLOCK WEIR 865478. Sheltered by Worthy Woods, it looks across Porlock Bay to Hurlstone Point. With tiny harbour, pebbled beach, old inn and large car park.

RALEIGH'S CROSS 039344. On Brendon Hills with inn of long standing.

ROADWATER 035385. Pop. about 350. Together with Washford it is in the parish of Old Cleeve. Several turnings off the A.39 lead to this long straggling village and on into the Brendons.

ROBBER'S BRIDGE 820465. Narrow bridge over Weir Water in Oare valley. Favourite picnic spot with large car park recently made.

ROBIN HOWE 908428. Road from Webber's Post to Dunkery Gate climbs between Robin Howe, 1,403 feet, and Dunkery Beacon, 1,705 feet.

RODHUISH 017396. Hamlet in parish of Carhampton, and an old Domesday manor. Its name means 'dwelling place of the radman or judge'.

SELWORTHY 920468. Pop. 556. Famous village of thatched cottages, early church, and extensive views to Dunkery. Largely owned by National Trust. Small car park opposite church.

SHOULSBARROW CASTLE 705391. Rectangular Iron Age fort on the ridge between High Bray and Challacombe.

SIMONSBATH 775394. Pop. 234. Throughout the last century associated with the Royal Forest and Knight family. Now a quiet hamlet by the Barle, and centre of Exmoor parish. B.3223 approach over moors from Lynton is most impressive.

SOUTH MOLTON 715260. Pop. 2,993. Early Closing Wednesday. Market Day Thursday. This 'town on the Mole', as the name implies, is six miles beyond S. border of the National Park. A busy and ancient market town serving much of S.W. Exmoor. Attractive Guildhall, museum, and church. Two miles to N.W. is Shallowford House where Henry Williamson lived. Sheep Fair, last Thursday in August.

STOKE PERO 878435. Pop. 32. A scattered hamlet of some nine farms. The small church at 1,013 feet claims to be highest on Exmoor. Its date and dedication are lost but list of incumbents begins in 1242 with 'John, parson of Stoke'. The name 'Pero' derives from a family who held land here about 1300.

TARR STEPS 868322. Ancient causeway over Barle, and the finest of its kind in the country. Best approached by turning off B.3223 Winsford Hill. Large car park and toilets.

TIMBERSCOMBE 956420. Pop. 359. The village is partly sheltered within a valley on A.396. Its Saxon name means 'wooded valley'. To the W. is Bickham Manor, called in the Domesday survey 'Bichecome'.

TIVINGTON 934451. A hamlet in parish of Selworthy on the winding road to Wootton Courtenay. The 15th century thatched church of St. Leonard's is a chapel of ease. At one time it was adapted as a cottage, and an occupied cottage is still attached to E. end.

TREBOROUGH 010364. Pop. 44. Consists of a small, plain church and a few buildings exposed 1,000 feet up on N.E. Brendons. Once had important slate quarries. Name means, 'Place of waterfall'.

TRENTISHOE 646486. Pop. 47. Tiny hamlet not far from mouth of river Heddon. Until the chancel was added the church was reckoned the smallest in Devon. Still has its musicians' gallery.

TWITCHEN 790305. Pop. 81. Hamlet of a few farms and houses around the church of St. Peter. Situated among the hills on S. border of National Park. Rookery in the churchyard beeches.

UPTON 994290. Pop. 133. Small village along B.3190 on N.E. edge of Haddon Hill. Ruined tower of old church a mile away amid trees. Its bells and Norman font lie unused in a new building.

VALLEY OF THE ROCKS 705496. Famous beauty spot one mile W. of Lynton. A rocky amphitheatre 700 feet above sea. Car Park.

WATERSMEET 744487. Beauty spot at junction of East Lyn river with Hoaroak Water 1½ miles from Lynmouth. Limited parking opposite on A.39.

WEBBER'S POST 903440. Popular view point among conifers overlooking Horner Woods. Plenty of parking space on this National Trust land.

WHEDDON CROSS 925388. On crest of Dunster—Dulverton road almost opposite Dunkery Beacon. Nearly 1,000 feet high with 'Rest and Be Thankful' inn. In parish of Cutcombe.

WHIT STONES 853464. Two ancient stones, once on the Forest boundary, just S. of road near top of Porlock Hill. Legend says they were thrown in a contest between the devil and a giant.

WINSFORD 905350. Pop. 363. Pretty village set in wide valley amid wooded hills, and best reached from a turning off A.396. At the junction of Winn brook and river Exe. Has a famous thatched inn, the Royal Oak, and pleasant tea rooms. Ernest Bevin, the Labour statesman, was born here.

WINSFORD HILL 875343. Open heather moor belonging to National Trust with extensive Exmoor views. Crossed by B.3223 Dulverton—Exford road and crowned by Wambarrows, 1,404 feet. See also Caratacus Stone.

WITHIEL FLOREY 987334. Pop. about 30. Parish of scattered farms and 15th century church amid the green fields of the Brendons.

WITHYCOMBE 015413. Pop. 345. Village of many old cottages and most interesting church. Largely unknown to the thousands of tourists rushing into Minehead on A.39 less than a mile away. Named from the withies or willows which still flourish in village stream.

WITHYPOOL 845356. Pop. 252. A rather isolated village on river Barle mentioned in Domesday Book. Named, like Withycombe, from the willows of the river. Handsome five-arched bridge, and church dedicated to St. Andrew. Walter Raymond lived in a cottage here, 1905-14, writing books on Somerset life. R. D. Blackmore also wrote part of *Lorna Doone* in the Royal Oak inn.

WOODY BAY 675490. On the narrow cliff road five miles W. of Lynton. Scattered dwellings and hotel set among oak woodlands that reach right down to sea. Beach and landing place.

WOOTTON COURTENAY 938434. Pop. 265. The village stretches for more than a mile along lower S.W. slope of Grabbist. Fine views up to Dunkery range. Named from John de Courtenay, who held the manor in Norman days. Some wonderful carved bosses in roof of All Saints church.

Ivy-leaved Crowfoot.

8 Further Reading

An Exmoor Bibliography will be found in *The Exmoor Review* 1972, 35p. post free, from the Exmoor Society, Dulverton.

Books listed below have been divided into two sections: I. Those currently in print and available in most bookshops. II. Some important works which can be obtained only through County Libraries or second-hand bookshops.

1. Books Currently in Print

Allen, N. V. *The Birds of Exmoor.* Exmoor Press, 1971.

Blackmore, R. D. *Lorna Doone.* Various publishers.

Bourne, H. L. *Living on Exmoor.* Galley Press, 1963.

Burton, S. H. *Exmoor.* Hodder and Stoughton, 1970.

Dent, Anthony A. *The Pure Bred Exmoor Pony.* Exmoor Press, 1970.

The Exmoor Review. Annually since 1959. Many numbers are still available from The Exmoor Society, Parish Rooms, Dulverton.

Farr, G. *Ships and Harbours of Exmoor.* Exmoor Press, 1970.

Grinsell, L. V. *The Archaeology of Exmoor.* David and Charles, 1970.

Hurley, J. E. *Murder and Mystery on Exmoor.* Exmoor Press, 1971.

Hurley, J. E. *Snow and Storm on Exmoor.* Exmoor Press, 1972.

Lloyd, E. R. *The Wild Red Deer of Exmoor.* Exmoor Press, 1970.

Madge, R. *Railways Round Exmoor.* Exmoor Press, 1971.

Maund, H. B. *The Fish of Exmoor.* Exmoor Press, 1970.

Miles, R. *The Trees and Woods of Exmoor.* Exmoor Press, 1972.

Orwin, C. S., and Sellick, R. *The Reclamation of Exmoor Forest.* David and Charles, 1970.

Peel, J. H. B. *Portrait of Exmoor.* Hale, 1970.

Sinclair, G. *The Vegetation of Exmoor.* Exmoor Press, 1970.

Wedlake, A. L. *A History of Watchet.* Exmoor Press, 1973.

Whybrow, C. *Antiquary's Exmoor.* Exmoor Press, 1970.

II. Other Important Works

Chadwyck-Healey, C. E. H. *The History of Part of West Somerset.* Sotheran, 1901.

Collinson, J. *The History and Antiquities of the County of Somerset.* Crutwell, 1791.

Collyns, C. P. *Notes on the Chase of the Wild Red Deer.* Longman, Green, Longman and Roberts, 1862.

Hancock, The Rev. F. *The Parish of Selworthy.* Barnicott, 1897.

Hendy, E. W. *Wild Exmoor Through The Year.* Cape, 1930.

Hoskins, W. G. *Devon.* Collins, 1954.

MacDermot, E. T. *History of the Forest of Exmoor.* Wessex Press, 1911.

Maxwell-Lyte, H. C. *History of Dunster.* St. Catherine's Press, 1909.

Risdon, T. *Survey of Devon.* Rees and Curtis, 1811.

Savage, J. *History of the Hundred of Carhampton.* Strong, 1830.